£14·95

636.10092
NEW

MILTON

MILTON

Gillian Newsum

 The Kenilworth Press

ACKNOWLEDGEMENTS

Many people have helped me in the research for this book, but in particular I would like to thank Doreen Bradley, John Whitaker and Steve Hadley. I am also grateful to those riders and officials who have contributed comments about Milton, and to John Harding-Rolls and Fergus Graham for their information on his breeding.

PICTURE CREDITS

Terry Begg, courtesy *Horse and Pony*: 81, 93; Martin Dalby: 36, 39; Werner Ernst: 55, 65; Elizabeth Furth: 24, 29, 32, 40, 59, 67 (right), 74, 88, 90; Jan Gyllensten: 10, 56 (both pictures), 87 (both pictures); John Harding-Rolls: 18 (both pictures); Kit Houghton: 27, 28, 46, 64, 66, 67 (left), 84; Bob Langrish: 6, 9, 12, 31, 34 (both pictures), 45, 48, 51, 52-53, 71, 80, 83 (top); Peter Llewellyn, Photosport France: 60; Marcia MacLeod: 83 (bottom); Trevor Meeks, courtesy *Horse and Hound*: endpapers, 2, 58, 61, 62, 63, 69, 78, 86; Monty: 13 (both pictures); J. Mudd: 19; MVR Photographic: 16; Cornelia Nordström, Pressens Bild AB: 54, 82; Sally Anne Thompson, Animal Photography: 43, 44; Elisabeth Weiland: 35.

First published in 1991 by
The Kenilworth Press Ltd
Addington
Buckingham
MK18 2JR

© The Kenilworth Press Ltd, 1991

British Library Cataloguing in Publication Data

Newsum, Gillian
  Milton.
  I. Title
  798.25

  ISBN 1872082203

Designed by Phil Kay
Typeset in 11pt ITC Garamond by
DP Photosetting, Aylesbury, Bucks
Printed and bound by
Butler & Tanner, Frome, Somerset

CONTENTS

Foreword by John Whitaker, MBE

When I had Ryan's Son I thought it was unlikely that I would ever find another horse as good as him, so to have one that is even better makes me feel quite spoilt. Milton is the sort of horse you come across once in a lifetime, and I am lucky to have had the chance to ride him.

One of Milton's best assets is that he can sense the important occasions; he always responds well to a big audience and a tense atmosphere. My best moment with him was when we won the individual title at the European Championships in Rotterdam in 1989. Until then I had come second so many times in the really big competitions that I was beginning to think I would never win one, so to take the gold medal in Rotterdam meant more to me than anything else.

I am very pleased that this book has been written about Milton. Looking through the text and photographs brings back a lot of happy memories.

INTRODUCTION

'Majestic Milton'; 'Milton, show jumping's wonder horse'; 'Milton the magnificent'; 'Marvellous Milton' – never have so many superlatives been heaped upon one horse. Wherever he goes, in Britain or abroad, Milton is greeted with rapturous acclaim; the young and pony-mad treat him like an equine pop star – they collect posters of their hero and wear 'I love Milton' badges – and the star himself is the recipient of an endless stream of fan mail. In the history of show jumping no horse has ever been the subject of such universal admiration.

It is not just Milton's ability to out-jump his rivals that makes him so popular: he has a presence, an almost magical aura about him, when he comes into an arena – a dramatic combination of near-white colour, extravagant movement and controlled power. Everything he does seems to be in slow motion with an unusual action that makes him look like a rocking-horse come to life.

Like a good actor, he has the ability to draw the attention of his audience and then to hold it throughout his performance. The bigger the audience, the more inspired is his performance. He loves jumping and he loves the atmosphere of a crowded indoor arena; and when the pressure is on, he is in his element.

Milton has won nearly every major Grand Prix; he has European team and individual gold medals to his name; he has won the World Cup Final for two consecutive years; he took the individual silver medal at the World Championships in Stockholm; he has dominated the lucrative International Masters competition at Wembley's Horse of the Year Show and, during his career, has won over £900,000 in prize-money.

As well as being an inspiration to show jumping enthusiasts throughout the world, he is also a fitting memorial to the woman who first discovered him and who had so much faith in his potential. Caroline Bradley bought Milton for £1000 when he was only six months old. Six years later, in 1983, she died after collapsing in the collecting ring at the Suffolk County Show. Now, when Milton wins a class, it is not only a popular victory but another reminder of the brilliant and dedicated horsewoman who gave Milton such a valuable start to his career.

Milton is lucky always to have been in the hands of careful, sympathetic riders. Steve Hadley looked after him soon after Caroline's death, and in 1985 he went to his current rider, John Whitaker. It is John who has brought out the best in him. There is a fine line between allowing a horse like Milton to enjoy his superstar status and 'keeping him in his place. In his quiet, subtle way John has been able to tread this line to the benefit of both of them. He has had to adapt to Milton's style, not vice versa, but in doing so he has gained the horse's confidence to such an extent that Milton will always listen and respond to his aids. The horse is obedient, but he has lost none of his natural exuberance; and it is that enthusiasm for the sport, that desire to clear every fence, that has given Milton his superstar qualities.

Milton with his owners, Mr and Mrs Tom Bradley.

9

1.

Early Life

Considering that until recently the breeding of performance horses in Britain has tended to be a somewhat hit-and-miss affair, the British are lucky to be able to claim responsibility for producing the greatest show jumper in the world – there can be few who would argue with that attribution to Milton. Many of Britain's top show jumpers have no traceable pedigree and, as yet, there is no national registration system, but Milton was actually the result of a serious attempt by a British breeder to produce horses specifically for show jumping.

Even so, his pedigree gave only an inkling of the extraordinary talent that he would possess. It had not been expected to produce such a phenomenal result – indeed the match between his parents was never repeated, the mare being sold on soon after Milton was born, so there are no full brothers or sisters to Milton. His father was the stallion Marius, who had been imported to Britain from Holland as a three-year-old by Fergus Graham. With the late Caroline Bradley riding him, Marius achieved much success, including victory in the Queen Elizabeth II Cup in 1978.

Milton's mother was a half-bred mare called Epauletta, who produced Milton when she was only four years old and therefore before she had shown any form in the show jumping ring. When she did compete, her best achievement was seventh place in the 1983 Foxhunter Championship, and soon afterwards she was sold to the Belgian dealer François Mathy as a broodmare. Derek Ricketts, who rode Epauletta as a novice (and changed her name to Aston Answer), regarded her as a good, honest mare and a very careful jumper, but not exceptional. 'It's surprising how Milton got his scope. Marius was good, but he couldn't jump half the things that Milton can, and Aston Answer didn't strike me as having tremendous scope.'

Aston Answer was, however, from a fairly good line of jumpers. Her mother, Pennywort, won the Foxhunter Championship in 1970, although she was not the easiest of horses to ride, being a highly strung mare, and she had her limitations. After her victory at Wembley it was decided to breed from her. Aston Answer's sire, Any Questions, was a seven-parts thoroughbred who had done well in show jumping, dressage and one-day events.

Milton's arrival was orchestrated by John Harding-Rolls, an enthusiastic horseman who, with the help of Fergus Graham, set up a stud specifically to breed show jumpers.

He takes up the story:

Marius, Milton's father, with whom Caroline Bradley won the Queen Elizabeth II Cup at the Royal International Horse Show in 1978.

'It would be true to say that the breeding of Milton was in response to a challenge good-humouredly thrown down to me by Fergus Graham in the summer of 1970. [He had said that it was difficult to breed a show jumper.] In reply, I asked him whether the confluence of several lines of jumping stock could not produce one.

I had just agreed to buy Pennywort from Margaret Oxby for Paula Graham [Fergus's wife] to jump. Pennywort, by Top Walk, was a breedy sort of mare and Paula managed to get quite a tune out of her. Paula persevered with her jumping throughout the season and was rewarded for this by winning the coveted Foxhunter Championship in October from West Side Story with Caroline Bradley up and True Lass ridden by Harvey Smith. True Lass was bought into the stud a few weeks later, and with her Caroline became the first woman to win the Berliner Bär.

At my instigation, Fergus started looking for a suitable stallion and some

Pennywort, Milton's granddam, who won the 1970 Foxhunter Championships with Paula Graham.

Any Questions, Milton's grandsire, ridden by Paula Graham. He was a good all-rounder.

MILTON'S PEDIGREE

Although Milton is almost half thoroughbred, he has a great mixture of other bloodlines including Arab (going back to Shagya-Basa on his dam's side, through Any Questions), and Oldenburg, Holstein, Trakehner, and Groningen, all from Marius's side. The Groningen (which comes from Marius's great grandsire Camillus) was the traditional Dutch farm horse, heavy in type with a long back, flat croup and high knee action, and it was used mostly for carriage work. The refining qualities have come from the warmbloods, such as the Trakehner, and the Thoroughbred.

Marius (Milton's sire) – Originally called Middle Road because he was thought to be by the Irish stallion Middle Temple, his true identity as a Dutch Warmblood was proven later. He was not graded with the Dutch Warmblood Society as a three-year-old because, at 16hh, he would probably have been considered too small; and as he was never presented to the British Warmblood Society for blood-typing, so none of his progeny can be registered. However, his breeding is impressive and he has produced other good performance horses.

His own performance record includes the Queen Elizabeth II Cup (1978), the Grand Prix at the Birmingham Spring Show (1979) and the Leading Show Jumper of the Year Championship at Wembley (1977) with the late Caroline Bradley.

Marco Polo (Marius's sire) – Born in 1965, in Germany, and died in 1976. He was quite a small horse but produced some excellent jumpers and also three other famous stallions – Legaat, Recruit and Irco Polo. The latter, crossed with the Irish-bred mare Ballymena Park, who was exported to Sweden, has sired some outstanding performance horses, including the international show jumper Marcoville, who was ridden on the Swedish team at the World Championships in Stockholm in 1990.

Sinaeda (Marius's grandsire) – He had interesting breeding, being by Camillus ($\frac{3}{4}$ Groningen and $\frac{1}{4}$ Oldenburg) out of the famous Holstein mare Morgenster, who was one of the most influential mares imported from Germany into Holland. The eldest of Morgenster's graded sons, Senator (by Paladijn), is the grandsire of Nimmerdor, regarded as the greatest of the modern Dutch stallions. Apollo, Nick Skelton's famous show jumper, is also a descendant of Sinaeda.*

* Information on the Dutch breeding was taken from *The International Warmblood Horse*, by Celia Clarke and Debbie Wallin (Kenilworth Press).

Aston Answer (Milton's dam) – A 16.2hh grey mare originally called Epauletta, she was bred by John Harding-Rolls from Fergus Graham's stallion Any Questions, and she produced Milton when she was four years old. She began her show jumping career with Derek Ricketts, and was later sold to Mrs Elizabeth Dodwell (née Ahlström). She was an honest, careful jumper, and reached the Foxhunter Final at Wembley in 1983, where she finished seventh. She was later sold to the Belgian dealer François Mathy as a broodmare, and is now owned by Mr J.M. Dechamps at the Haras du Rezidal in Belgium.

Milton was the only foal that Aston Answer bred in this country, but with her new owners she has produced two colts. The first, Eaton, by Furisto, is now an approved stallion in Belgium, and one of the mares he covered in 1991 is Concern, the full sister to Big Ben (Ian Millar's World Cup Final winner in 1988 and 1989). Aston Answer's second foal is Greeton, by Galant de la Cour. Both progeny are grey like their dam. In 1991 Aston Answer was put in foal to Vondel, son of Widukind, who is a good performance stallion belonging to Eric Wauters.

Any Questions (Aston Answer's sire) – A 16.1hh light-weight, grey stallion, seven-eighths thoroughbred. He was not a particularly careful jumper but had a good temperament and was tough. He competed in the Foxhunter Championships, performed well in dressage and eventing, and was hunted regularly with the Bicester. He was later exported to Sweden, where he died at the age of twenty-three.

Pennywort (Milton's granddam) – She had good bone and was a careful jumper, but lacked scope and was not particularly bold. She won the Foxhunter Championship in 1970 before being put in foal to Any Questions. Her first foal by Any Questions died as a three-year-old, after being struck by lightning, but her second was Epauletta (Aston Answer). She produced other good horses including Hypericum (by Marius) who, under the new name of Jameel, became a leading show jumper in Oman. Two more of her offspring, Penmar (by Marius) and Penduo (by the German stallion Grandeur) are also show jumpers.

Top Walk (Pennywort's sire) – A thoroughbred stallion with a respectable racing record. During his career, which spanned six years, he had fifteen wins out of sixty-five starts, and was either second or third on twenty-five other occasions. He proved to be a sound horse with a good temperament, and he sired a number of good horses, including three Wembley champions in 1970: Foxhunter champion Pennywort, hunter champion Top Notch, and champion police horse Pennine Way.

14

MILTON					
MARIUS	MARCO POLO (1496)	POET (XX)	JANITOR	FERVOR	
				JANE PERNEY	
			PRISKA	HEROD	
				PREISFRAGE	
		MIRAKEL (1882 Trak)	ALTAN	HIRTENSANG	
				AMCANTE	
			MIRA	LOWENHERTZ	
				MYSTIK	
	OMINKA (35848 B)	SINAEDA (1412)	CAMILLUS	CAMBINUS	
				ANITA	
			MORGENSTER (Holst)	GABRIËL	
				BANKA	
		RAMINKA (27935 B)	FEINER KERL (Old)	FÜRST	
				UTANIE III	
			FREIMINKA (Old)	GODIN	
				FREIHEIT II	
ASTON ANSWER (EPAULETTA)	ANY QUESTIONS	QUESTIONNAIRE	CALIPH	SHAGYA-BASA (Arab)	
				CHOCOLATE CREAM (XX)	
			SWEET BRIAR (XX)	FIELD TRIAL	
				NORTON ROSE	
		SEINE (XX)	RIVER PRINCE	ROSE PRINCE	
				VIESTE	
			FRENCH PARTRIDGE	SALAMIS	
				FRENCH MARTEN	
	PENNYWORT	TOP WALK (XX)	CONCERTO	ORPHEUS	
				CONSTELLATION	
			PHALARA'S FIRST	PHALARA	
				SELF-BINDER	
		LUCKY PENNY (Hunter)	PENANCE	PENITENT	
				SISTER MARY	
			LUCKY GIRL	ASTRA	
				LADY LUCK	

XX = Thoroughbred; Holst = Holstein; Old = Oldenburg; Trak = Trakehner

15

Epauletta (by now renamed Aston Answer) competing in the 1983 Foxhunter Championship at the Horse of the Year Show with Clare Jones. She finished in seventh place after collecting 8 faults in the final jump-off.

hunters for me to ride. Several hunters, all by Middle Temple and out of mares by Lansdowne and Surish, and a half-bred stallion, which I named Lord Thomas, were bought off the late Archie Thomlinson of Grewelthorpe in Yorkshire. I was further advised to buy the mare Randallstown Hills, better known as Tiffany, Alan Oliver's mount; and a small stallion [called Middle Road], by Middle Temple out of a Connemara pony mare [or so Fergus Graham had been told].

I clearly recollect saying to Fergus at the time that there did not seem to be any Middle Temple stamp about him, with which he rather reluctantly agreed. However, I continued to call him Middle Road up until his first appearance, ridden by Caroline Bradley, at Wembley in the Foxhunter Championship [which he failed to win after a muddle over the course for the jump-off]. It was here that, if my memory serves me correctly, Eric Wauters, Johan Heins and Ted Edgar recognised him as a Dutch-bred stallion. Fergus discovered that his real name was Marius [and that he had full Dutch warmblood papers], and I decided at once to correct the mistake.

To acknowledge the help given to me by Fergus and Paula Graham I presented them with Pennywort's first foal by their stallion Any Questions. Sadly, it did not survive. Pennywort's second foal I named Epauletta, for Paula. As a three-year-old she was put to Marius and produced a colt foal which I named Marius Silver Jubilee [now Milton], a name that indicated his sire, his colour and his age. This colt was sold to Caroline for £1000 as a weanling in December 1977; she thought the price a bit steep, and indeed to achieve £1000 for a half-bred weanling whose dam had never performed was good going in those days.'

John Harding-Rolls continues to breed show jumpers at the Marius-Milton Stud in Stratton Audley, Oxfordshire, and has Marius's son and grandson standing at stud. Other successful progeny from Marius includes the international three-day eventer Master Marius; and his own jumping record was considerable: he won the Grand Prix at the Birmingham Spring Show and the Leading Show Jumper of the Year title at Wembley, as well as the Queen Elizabeth II Cup. It is from Marius, who died in December 1986, that Milton has inherited much of his character. Nicknamed 'Dennis the Menace' on the yard because he would rip off his rug and bandages if his breakfast was late, Caroline used to say that if she could get Marius past the tenth fence without faults then she had a chance of winning. He suffered from asthma all his life so he had to be bedded on peat and have his hay steamed, and at night he always had an infra-red lamp on in his box.

When Epauletta (Aston Answer) was put to Marius she produced Milton in the spring of 1977. A year later she was sold, just broken-in, to Derek Ricketts. 'I nearly bought her foal as well,' recalls Derek, 'but I was told that Caroline wanted him, so I just took the mare.' He changed her name to Aston Answer because most of his horses carried the Aston prefix (Derek lived near Aston Abbotts, Buckinghamshire) and the second part of her name tied in well with her father being Any Questions. He produced her as a novice, winning a few Foxhunter classes, before selling her to Elizabeth Ahlström (now Mrs Dodwell), who was based with the trainer Lars Sederholm, at Waterstock. Together with Clare Jones, Elizabeth jumped Aston Answer at local shows, and Clare rode her in the 1983 Foxhunter Championship, where she had 8 faults in the final jump-off and finished seventh.

Her foal had been earmarked by Caroline at the age of six months; she liked the look of him and also had a high regard for his breeding. Once she had bought 'the little grey thing', as he soon became known to the Bradleys, she changed his name from Marius Silver Jubilee to Milton because she liked to call all her horses after local villages near her home at Priors Marston, Warwickshire. 'I remember seeing him when he arrived,' recalls Doreen Bradley, Caroline's mother. 'He looked like a dark grey 13.2hh pony. Caroline used to tell us not to mock the little grey thing, as he was going to be the best show jumper ever.'

She was right, but tragically did not live to see her prediction come true. She had gone no further than training Milton as a youngster and guiding him through his first small competitions before she died.

Caroline had an exceptional talent for training young horses. She was patient and dedicated, and always did her utmost to get the best out of a horse. During her association with John Harding-Rolls she jumped sixteen of his horses, and she also brought on youngsters for the German rider and trainer Paul Schockemöhle. Caroline owned only a handful of the horses she rode, but she did have a half share in Tigre, the horse on whom she achieved her greatest

Milton with his mother Epauletta (Aston Answer). Epauletta was only four years old when Milton was born in 1977, and she did not have any other foals in this country.

Caroline Bradley jumping Milton as a novice five-year-old at Moulsoe in September 1982. Caroline died the following year.

successes. Even that was no guarantee of security, however; she eventually lost the ride on him after nearly a year of heartbreaking negotiations with his joint-owner Donald Bannocks.

In 1981, when Tigre eventually left Caroline's yard, she had no outstanding Grade A horses to replace him. Milton, the one really talented horse that she owned outright, was still a novice four-year-old. However, she already knew that she had an exceptional horse in Milton: 'Every time I jump him he goes higher and higher,' she told her mother. 'If he's put under pressure he just goes up.' He won nearly every time he went out, so Caroline's most serious problem was trying to keep him at the appropriate level, otherwise he would upgrade too quickly for his own good.

Like his father, Milton had been a rather boisterous youngster. Yorkshire-man Bill Brown, who broke him in for Caroline as a three-year-old, had found him quite a handful, and on the yard at home he had been nicknamed 'Hitler', because he was so bossy. 'He cost us a small fortune in rugs and rollers,' recalls Mrs Bradley. 'Caroline was a great believer in anti-cast rollers, using them on all her top horses, but if Milton felt like it he could blow out his stomach so much that he would burst the roller.' He was also (and still is) a master at removing his rug in one piece. No one has ever discovered how he does it, but unless the rug has straps around the legs, he can pull it off over his head. 'It's another trait he's inherited from his father,' says Mrs Bradley. 'Except that Marius used to take his rugs off in bits.'

When Milton was two years old a curious incident occurred at the Bradley's yard. The groom arrived one morning to find not a single friendly face looking out over the stable doors. 'All the horses in the inner yard had been poisoned,' explained Mrs Bradley. Caroline was away at the Birmingham Spring Show at the time, and she came home afterwards to find three dead horses, and nine others so ill that they were in danger of dying.

Milton had been in the field at the time, out of harm's way, but about two weeks after the tragedy someone in the village rang the Bradleys to say that there was another dead horse in the field. They rushed out to find 'Hitler' lying prostrate on the grass – he was having a nap in the hot afternoon sun.

Milton was six years old when Caroline died. He was a Grade B jumper at that time, but still very inexperienced, the extent of his travels being only two nights away from home. Caroline had taken him to the Royal Cornwall Show, and then to the Suffolk County Show, Ipswich. It was while they were there, in June 1983, that Caroline, who was thirty-seven years old, collapsed after competing in the main class. She died on the way to hospital.

Stress and overwork were almost certainly the main causes of her death, which stunned the show jumping world. A tribute in *The Times* read: 'Without doubt she was far and away the most outstanding woman rider of show jumpers in the world. . . . She was a pattern for young aspirants and she will be quite irreplaceable.'

Caroline had made her international debut in 1966, when she was twenty, and had remained one of the key riders on the British team for seventeen years. She had represented Britain on twelve winning Nations Cup teams, and was a member of the gold medal team at the 1978 World Championships and the 1979 European Championships. In 1974 she had created history by becoming the first woman to win the Puissance at the Horse of the Year Show, and the following year had an outstanding victory in the Hamburg Derby, coming first with New Yorker and second with Acrobat.

At the time of her death there were twenty-nine horses on the yard, eleven of them jumping. 'When you have had the rug pulled from under your feet you cannot adjust straight away,' said Mrs Bradley. 'We decided to do nothing for six weeks to give ourselves a chance to do some planning, so we told the girls to feed down the horses and just exercise them each day.' The Bradleys had thought initially that they would try to keep the yard going, but soon realised this was not feasible. Many of the horses went back to their owners, and Milton was offered to John Whitaker.

At the moment that the Bradleys rang John to ask if he would like to try Milton, he had a lorry full of horses about to leave for Scotland. They were going to the Royal Highland Show and then on to Glasgow, a round trip of two weeks, so John asked if he could try Milton when he got back. Alas, by the time he had

Milton with Steve Hadley at Newbury Show in 1983. Not long after this show Milton cut his tendon while being clipped and did not compete again for nearly two years.

returned home and contacted the Bradleys again, it was too late; Milton had gone to Steve Hadley. In his usual nonchalant manner John just shrugged his shoulders and dismissed his misfortune: 'What you've never had you don't miss.'

The first time John had seen Milton was at Rufforth Park, near Wetherby, Yorkshire, when, as a four-year-old, he had looked promising. But later on, when he saw him competing with Steve Hadley, he was not that impressed: 'At the time I didn't think I'd really missed much,' he says.

Steve Hadley, on the other hand, knew that he had got hold of something special. 'Once I had jumped him it was obvious to me he was going to be exceptional. He was in a different class from anything I had ever ridden before, and I've had some nice horses. It was the feeling he gave you when he came off the ground, his extravagant action. He was so elastic. As a six-year-old he could do flying changes without any effort, and he had such a big jump. At that age I never did any really big fences on him, but you could always feel that you'd got another foot and a half to come.'

Within two months of arriving at Steve Hadley's yard Milton was in Grade A classes. 'He kept on jumping clear rounds,' explains Steve. 'He had so much ability.' By early September of that year he was competing in the £500 classes at shows like Thame, Camberley and Henley. He then went to Park Farm, which at that time was a regular pre-Wembley show, and competed against some of the top Grade A horses; he jumped double clear rounds on all three days.

Steve Hadley has tremendous respect for the work that Caroline had done on him. 'She produced him beautifully and taught him his trade. I remember watching her riding him in the Grade C Championships at the Royal International [1982], where she jumped a double clear, but didn't win because she never set fire to him against the clock. I tried to do the same thing. I jumped a lot of double clears with him, but didn't win many classes because there wasn't any point in pushing him against the clock at that stage. You get all the joy with a horse like that in just jumping a clear round and doing it the right way.'

Milton obviously had outstanding ability, but as a young horse he might easily have been passed over for being too careless. He had a tendency to dangle his front legs, which could cause problems, particularly at verticals. 'If he had got into bad hands as a youngster and been made to do things prematurely, he might have suddenly decided he didn't like the job any more,' says Steve Hadley. 'But by being ridden consistently in the correct way by a skilful rider, as Caroline was, he had a good platform from which to work, and he could find his feet and learn to do the job in his own time.'

After a successful three months around the summer shows with Steve, Milton had a month off. The intention was to take him to Olympia in December to compete in the smaller classes, for although he was only six at the time, Steve thought him capable of handling that level of competition. But Milton never got to Olympia. While Steve was competing at the annual international show in Dubai he had a call from his wife, Clare, to say that Milton was injured.

Milton had always been difficult to clip. Normally a friendly soul in his box, the sight of clippers (or a syringe) sends him beserk. 'He would kick you out of the box if you weren't careful,' recalls Steve. On this occasion he was only having his heels trimmed in preparation for Olympia, but he suddenly reared up and struck out. 'We don't know to this day whether he hit the blade of the clippers with his leg or whether he struck into himself with his other leg.' Whatever happened, the result was a cut in Milton's near fore tendon.

At first the injury was thought to be superficial, but when it failed to heal up satisfactorily Geoffrey Braine, from Bourton-on-the-Water, a vet much admired by Caroline, was consulted. It transpired that the wound was deeper than anyone had realised, and the tendon was quite seriously damaged. Geoffrey Braine decided to perform a split tendon operation on Milton, whereby the fibres of the tendon are separated slightly to encourage stronger growth as the tendon heals, and he was hobdayed at the same time because Steve Hadley had noticed that he made a noise in his wind.

Milton went back to Priors Marston to convalesce, and Steve went to visit him most days to check on his progress. After a year's rest the Bradleys moved him up into the field beside their new house, just above the village, where there was a steep hill (covered in snow at the time) on which Milton could exercise his muscles. 'It was all part of the treatment,' says Doreen Bradley, who got to know the horse quite well at that time. 'He was very good at opening gates, but not so good at gardening,' she recalls.

A couple of months later he went into livery with Evelyn England in Priors Hardwick so that he could be treated by Ronnie Longford, an expert on backs and limbs. There was still heat in his damaged leg, so he was given ultra-sonic treatment and kept stabled for a few weeks until the leg was completely cold (although even now there is still a slight thickening around the damaged tendon). Then he started light work, sometimes in a school because he was not particularly good in traffic and quite a 'sharp' ride, according to Evelyn. He did not let her forget that he was around in the stableyard either: 'Within an hour of arriving here he had broken a window in his stable. He was always up to something. But he was a wonderful ride. It was like riding a leaf. He was so light.' Unfortunately he was also very naughty. One day when Evelyn was trotting him quietly along the Feltway – a disused lane between Priors Hardwick and Priors Marston – he decided to spook at a piece of corrugated iron that he had seen hundreds of times before. He went straight up in the air, fell over backwards, and then cantered calmly home, leaving Evelyn to walk.

Soon after that incident it was considered time for Milton to move on, so the Bradleys consulted Paul Schockemöhle, who had been a very close friend of Caroline's. Paul had been involved in setting up the Next sponsorship for John and Michael Whitaker, and it was agreed that John should once more be asked if he would like to ride Milton. Caroline had always admired John's quiet, skilful riding, and she knew that he took great care of his horses. 'He's a very sympathetic rider,' says Mrs Bradley. 'You never see him losing his temper with a horse.' So this time John really did get Milton.

Although disappointed to lose such a good horse without warning, Steve Hadley understood the Bradley's decision. John Whitaker was on the international circuit and could take Milton to more shows, whereas Steve was beginning to wind down his international career and concentrate on training, commentating and journalism. 'It was obviously the right move for Milton. Very few people would believe me, but I honestly don't regret not having Milton. If he had stayed with me I would have felt obliged to keep going at international level for another seven or eight years, and I didn't want to be still competing on the circuit when I was fifty! I had Milton ten years too late.'

23

2.

International Debut

When Milton arrived at John Whitaker's yard in the bleak uplands of West Yorkshire, he was still relatively unfit. He had been off work for eighteen months, and although he had started walking and trotting exercise with Evelyn England, it was another two months before he was in a condition to attempt any jumping. 'He was quite fat,' recalls John, 'and if he had started jumping too soon he might have done some damage.' However, when John did eventually take him over his first jump, a low cross pole, Milton revealed his true colours: 'He must have cleared the pole by about three foot. You could feel the power and lightness. It was magic.'

It is not in the nature of this modest Yorkshireman to waste words, but on the subject of Milton he becomes quite loquacious. There is no doubt in his mind that Milton is the best horse he has ever sat on and that he is unlikely ever to come across another horse with such extraordinary talent. Even the great Ryan's Son, John's top horse for many years, did not have the scope and ability that Milton possesses, although he would jump his heart out to clear a big fence. 'Ryan was always struggling a bit in the really big classes. Milton has another gear. You feel you are never pushing Milton to his limits and that he's always got a little bit left in the tank.'

John, born on August 5, 1955, the eldest of four boys, began his show jumping career under the guidance of his mother, Enid, who encouraged all her children to ride on whatever ponies they could afford or could borrow from friends. The experience John gained on a large variety of often unsuitable ponies helped to develop his own natural ability to get the best from any horse, and it was not long before he began doing well in show jumping classes even with quite unpromising material. He made the transition from ponies to horses with a novice mare called Singing Wind, with whom he managed to qualify for Wembley. Then came Ryan's Son, who was bought for him by businessman Malcolm Barr. Mr Barr's daughter, Clare, went to work for the Whitakers in 1974 and became John's wife in 1979. They now have three children, Louise, Robert and Joanne, all keen riders.

With Ryan's Son, John worked his way up to international level. They soon established themselves as one of the top combinations in the country and became regular members of the British team, winning a team and individual silver medal at the 'Alternative Olympics' in Rotterdam, in 1980, and another team and individual silver medal at the 1983 European Championships. That year they also won the Hickstead Derby.

Milton competing at Rotterdam in 1986 during his first full year on the international circuit. Milton's style is exceptional: he brings his knees up so high in front that his legs are often higher than his tummy.

Before long, John had built up a strong team of horses which included Hopscotch, San Salvador and Gammon, and with Hopscotch he won the team gold and individual bronze medals at the 1985 European Championships. Earlier that year, at the World Cup final in Berlin, Paul Schockemöhle had approached John to see if he would be interested in taking on Milton. At that time John, together with his brother Michael, had just begun a six-year sponsorship agreement with Next, the clothing retailers, and Milton, though still inexperienced, would be a useful addition to his team.

So the eight-year-old, 'novice' Grade A jumper, was driven up to West Yorkshire to begin training with his new jockey. He arrived with certain conditions attached: he would not be available for the Olympics; he should not compete at the Suffolk County Show (where Caroline had died), and he should not be jumped in the Hickstead Derby. Apart from that, John could take his own decisions on where to ride Milton, and the Bradleys gave him an undertaking that if they ever took Milton away from him he would not be given to another rider in Britain.

However, before John could begin seriously competing on his new acquisition there was work to be done. Quite apart from getting the horse back into working condition, John had to learn how to cope with Milton's unusual style of jumping. Accustomed to horses like Ryan's Son, who was very sharp and quick off the ground coming into a fence, it seemed to John that Milton did everything in slow motion. This was because it took him so long to bring his front legs up underneath him and then stretch them out over the fence. Most horses tuck up their front legs straight away as they take off, but Milton lifts his up in an arc, gradually unfolding them out in front of him, with a slow, exaggerated action.

John describes the early days: 'When I rode him at his first shows he jumped quite well, but not brilliantly, and it took me a while to realise that he needed a lot of time to pick himself up in front of a fence. You had to sit very still when he was coming off the floor to give him time to use his front end.'

The technique for riding Milton was not obvious to start with, as John explains:

'Usually if a horse doesn't pick up his front legs well you need to bring him in a bit closer to the fence and ride him at it quicker, to make him use himself. I did this a couple of times with Milton, but it just made him worse, and he would twist over the fence. (Sometimes now if I am riding against the clock and I get a bit too close to a fence he will twist to get over it.) So I found out that I needed to stand him further back from a fence and give him more time to jump it.

'He had a long stride as well, which was part of the same problem. He had to learn to shorten, especially at combinations. Once he got confidence in me he was much better. Now he concentrates and listens to me, so if he needs to

Competing at Olympia in 1985. Olympia was only Milton's fourth international show, but in his previous three shows he had won a World Cup qualifier, come second in another, and finished third in a Grand Prix: a brilliant start to his international career.

shorten for a fence I can prepare him. He's very obedient – a bit like clockwork sometimes. The main thing is that he doesn't want to touch a fence, so he will always do his best to clear it.'

John, only 5ft 7ins, found the 16.2hh Milton quite strong to start with and decided to try him in a twisted snaffle, which he has used ever since. He does sometimes have trouble with his 'brakes', but can usually manage, and he sees little point in trying other bits when this one seems to work. Milton does have a habit, though, of rolling his tongue back and then leaning on the bit, so he is always ridden in a bit with cheeks, which are fastened back to the leather cheek-pieces of his bridle to keep the bit up in his mouth.

During their first summer together John did not jump Milton a great deal as he did not want to risk his injured leg on the hard ground. His first competition was at Leicester City, followed by an outing to their local show at Rotherham before the pre-Wembley show at Park Farm. As Milton had not qualified for Wembley, he had a short break before John took him on a trip to the Continent 'just to give him some experience', and they came home a month later having won a World Cup qualifier, come second in another, and finished third in a small Grand Prix. By the time the combination arrived at Olympia they were the talk of the show jumping circuit.

Competing at Olympia in 1986. 'His technique had improved,' says John. 'Initially I found that he would often over-jump to make sure that he cleared a fence, and sometimes his legs would be all over the place. He soon started to measure his fences better.'

'I had intended to take Milton into just the small classes at his first overseas shows, but he jumped everything so easily that each day I put him into a slightly more difficult class. He finished third in the small Grand Prix in Berlin, so when we went to Brussels, his next show, I decided to try him in the World Cup qualifier, where he came second. Then we went on to Bordeaux, where he won the World Cup qualifier. It wasn't a bad record for his first three outings at international level.' Milton had made the transition from local national shows to international level look easy.

At Olympia, however, the new partnership failed to make a significant impression. Milton, after his first trip abroad with three big shows in a row, was probably feeling a little weary and shell-shocked. His past experience of staying away at shows had been limited (he had been away only twice with Caroline), and he had certainly never travelled abroad before. Fortunately, though, he is not the sort of horse who frets on long journeys; his main concerns in life are eating and sleeping, and as long as he has plenty of both he is quite content.

Jumping the first element of the double on his way to winning the Grand Prix in Rotterdam in 1987. 'The others had gone quite fast against the clock, but they had had to slow up for the double to get in two strides,' explains John. 'I decided that the only way I could catch them was to keep going at the double and do it in one stride instead of two.'

The following year, 1986, Milton began his international career in earnest. He competed in Antwerp, Dortmund, Paris, S'Hertogenbosch, Windsor, Hickstead, South of England, Birmingham, Fontainebleau, Wolfsburg, Aachen, Royan, La Baule, Dinard, Rotterdam, Stockholm, Calgary, Wembley, Brussels, Bordeaux and Olympia.

His most valuable win of the year was the Calgary Grand Prix, worth £39,000 (it is worth a lot more now), which followed a successful outing for the British team in the Nations Cup competition in Calgary. It had been Milton's second Nations Cup performance; in his first, at Rotterdam a month earlier, he had made an impressive debut by jumping a double clear with just a fraction of a time fault in each round.

In Calgary the Nations Cup developed into a battle between the British and the Americans. Both countries finished the two rounds of the competition on 4 faults (both Milton and Nick Skelton's Apollo had jumped double clears for Britain), so there had to be a jump-off against the clock to find the winners. Milton produced a third clear round, with a fairly good time (35.56 secs), but, overall, the Americans were just 0.9 seconds faster than the British.

In the Grand Prix, Milton was one of four horses to get through to the jump-off against the clock. He then had another clear round, 7 seconds faster than the American, Laura Tidball-Balisky on Lavendal, which was good enough to give him victory when both Pierre Durand (with Jappeloup) and Markus Fuchs (with Pushkin) had fences down. By the end of that competition Milton had completed six consecutive clear rounds (including those in the Nations Cup) at this major international show.

Earlier in the year John had had a memorable time at the Royal International Horse Show at Birmingham. With his three horses – Ryan's Son, San Salvador and Milton – he had had only one fence down during the entire five days of the show. Milton was the culprit. He knocked one down on the first day, but he redeemed himself later by winning the Grand Prix against formidable opposition.

This was the same year that John won the King George V Gold Cup on Ryan's Son, who was then eighteen years old.

A month after Birmingham John took Milton to the World Championships in Aachen, as his second horse. He jumped so well there that John was tempted to put him into the championships instead of Hopscotch, but in the end decided against it. It would have been the biggest course that Milton had tackled in his short career, and it was not worth taking a risk with him at this stage.

Things were looking quite different by the end of the year, however. Milton had gained more experience at the big shows, where he had proved his ability and consistency, and there was little doubt that he would be included in the British team for the European Championships in St Gallen, Switzerland, in 1987.

The following summer Milton was duly selected, with Apollo (Nick

Jumping the water ditch at Hickstead in 1987. Milton had a fence down in the first round of the Nations Cup, followed by a clear in the second round (with 0.25 time faults).

Skelton), Angelzarke (Malcolm Pyrah) and Amanda (Michael Whitaker). It was a strong team, but no one had expected the British to score such an emphatic victory; they finished 25 points ahead of the closest contenders, France, and John and Milton narrowly missed winning the individual gold medal.

The conditions for the team competition in St Gallen were appalling. The ground was so wet that one of the German riders, Paul Schockemöhle (himself an individual European gold medallist on three occasions), tried to have the second leg, the Nations Cup, postponed. However, the competition went ahead, and the British horses coped well with the poor going.

Milton could probably have won the first leg, the speed competition, if John had taken the same turn as the Frenchman Pierre Durand with Jappeloup, going inside the water jump, but he decided the risk was too great. The going had deteriorated towards the end of the class, when Milton was drawn to go, so John played safe, jumped a clear round and finished the first leg in third place.

By the second day, when the team championship was decided, the ground had become even worse as a result of overnight and morning rain; there were pools of water all over the showground, and one end of the arena was completely waterlogged. The two fences sited there, a 5ft 2in vertical followed by a 5ft oxer, had become almost unjumpable by the second round of the Nations Cup.

However, Apollo, Anglezarke and Milton all jumped clear in the first round, putting Britain over 8 points ahead of France at the half way stage. In the second round Apollo jumped clear, and although Amanda collected 13.5 faults, Anglezarke's clear round gave Britain a good enough score to win the gold medal without John and Milton having to jump again. In a normal Nations Cup Milton could have gone back to the stable, but in a European Championships the faults are carried forward for the individual placings, so Milton had to jump the second round to establish his position. This he did in great style, despite the terrible state of the ground by that stage, and his second clear round (with just half a time fault) put him into third place for the start of the individual competition; Nick Skelton was lying second, and Pierre Durand first.

The conditions had altered dramatically for the final competition, which was held in bright sunshine on rapidly drying ground. Fortunately, Milton does not seem to mind what sort of going he jumps on, and he handled the changing conditions in St Gallen with little difficulty, producing his fourth successive clear round of the championships over the first of two massive courses for the individual competition. Only two others went clear, Thomas Frühmann with Porter, and Jappeloup. Apollo had one down, which dropped him to third place, while Milton edged up to second, just behind Jappeloup.

In the final round, where the fences were even bigger, Milton made his first mistake. It was at fence four, a narrow palisade stile, 5ft 3ins high, which caught out half the field. Uprights have always been a slight weakness with Milton (as

Jumping the water in Rotterdam, 1986. Milton has always been good at water jumps. The only time he has put a foot in the water was at the European Championships in 1989.

Hickstead, 1986. In his early competitions Milton's mane was always plaited, but he began shaking his head about when he was jumping, so John decided to stop plaiting him. 'I prefer him plaited,' says John, 'because it shows him off much better. But I don't think Milton liked it, and I used to find that the buttons on my jacket got caught up in the plaits, and then they would be pulled off.'

they often are with other horses) because they do not fill the eye as well as a large oxer, for example, and he sometimes lets his attention wander. That rail down in St Gallen lost him the gold medal. Jappeloup also had a fence down, so Milton would have won if he had gone clear.

Although it was a well-deserved and popular victory for the little French horse, it was a great disappointment for John. As Steve Hadley wrote in his *Horse and Hound* article: 'Let us spare a final thought for John Whitaker, who fought back to take the silver medal in these championships at Hickstead in 1983, led on the final day in Dinard two years later only to drop to bronze in the very last round, and did absolutely nothing wrong in St Gallen to finish with a silver again. It surely cannot be very long before a European Champion comes once more from this country.'

Steve Hadley was right. Two years later John and Milton did finally secure the individual gold medal at the European Championships in Rotterdam, but before then the partnership had gained numerous other victories.

All in all, 1987 had been a good year for Milton. He had won Grands Prix in Gothenburg and Rotterdam; he had jumped in eight Nations Cup competitions, gaining double clears in four of them (and in another two he had not needed to complete the second round); he had won the World Cup qualifier in New York, as well as classes in Paris, Hickstead, Dublin, Stuttgart, Toronto and Olympia. By the end of the year he had earned £91,742, making him Britain's top prize-money winner, a position he first gained in 1986 and has held ever since.

Steve Hadley

'Milton comes into his own when the fences get bigger and the other horses are beginning to struggle. The higher the level of jumping, the more chance he has of winning. That's why he does so well in the Masters at Wembley; when the fences get really big he finds another gear and starts to open up – he just goes higher and wider – whereas other horses are starting to close up and have a fence down. He has so much ability.'

Presentation time at the 1987 European Championships in St Gallen, Switzerland, where Milton and John won the individual silver medal and the British team won the gold. Milton can never resist food.

3.

Olympic Loss – European Victory

The year of the Seoul Olympics, 1988, was Milton's best so far, but his achievements were overshadowed by the furore that accompanied his exclusion from the Olympic Games. The British Show Jumping Association's selection committee, and many riders, members of the press and public found it difficult to accept that Doreen and Tom Bradley did not want Milton to go to Seoul, and the ensuing public debate left ill-feeling on either side. It was an unhappy time for everyone concerned, although Milton, blissfully unaware that he was the centre of so much media attention, continued to jump well at the major shows.

He had had a good start to the year, winning two World Cup qualifiers (Paris and S'Hertogenbosch) and the Grand Prix in Dortmund, Germany. By the end of the World Cup season, which runs from October to April with qualifiers all over the world, Milton was second in the European League, but at the final in Gothenburg he gave a disappointing performance in the first leg of the competition (the speed class), having two fences down. 'I think he probably peaked a bit too soon,' says John. However, Milton did jump one of only two clear rounds in the first jump-off of the second leg, which pulled him up considerably, and he eventually finished in eighth place.

After Dortmund there was a short rest before the Nations Cup meeting at Hickstead at the beginning of June, but by then the disquiet over Milton's Olympic team prospects had already begun. Officials at the BSJA tried to persuade the Bradleys to allow Milton to go to Seoul, but in the end Tom and Doreen Bradley stuck to the decision they had taken when they first gave the horse to John to ride.

The reasons they gave for not wishing Milton to go to the Olympics reflected their concern for his future, which was of paramount importance to them. Milton was their last link with Caroline and they wanted to preserve that link for as long as possible. A number of factors concerned with the Seoul Olympics were considered too great a risk for their horse – the length of journey, the possibility of the horse catching a deadly virus, and the knowledge that Olympic courses were often unnecessarily big. These reasons seemed fair enough, but others argued that the journey was shorter than that to Calgary, where Milton competes nearly every year, quarantine regulations had been carefully devised to avoid the possibility of the Olympic horses coming into contact with any viruses, and recent Olympic courses (particularly the previous one in Los Angeles, in 1984) had tended to be less demanding.

Looking composed as they jump neatly over the double oxer in the Grand Prix at the Royal International Horse Show, Birmingham (1988), where John and Milton did well despite the controversy over their omission from the Olympic team. They won the Daily Mail Cup on the opening night, were runners-up in the King George V Cup and won the Grand Prix.

The real reason for the Bradleys' decision went back much further, to before Milton was even born. In 1972, the year of the Munich Olympics, Caroline was having considerable success with a mare called Wood Nymph (by King of Diamonds). 'Caroline was asked if she would mind if Wood Nymph went to the Olympics,' explained Mrs Bradley. Caroline said she wouldn't, thinking that she would be the one to ride her. The next thing she heard was that the selectors wanted David Broome and Peter Robeson to try the mare. 'She didn't go well for either of them,' recalls Mrs Bradley, 'and Caroline was absolutely heartbroken watching them jump her. However, they said they wanted the horse for Munich, and that was that. Caroline had no means of stopping them. She cried and cried about it; and then pulled up her socks and became harder. She said to me afterwards: "That settles it. No horse of mine will ever go to the Olympics."'

Caroline never did compete in the Olympics. The following year, as a result of a decision by the International Equestrian Federation to straighten out the anomalies in the classification of amateur and professional show jumpers, she was forced to turn professional. She appealed against the decision on the grounds that, although she rode horses for other people, she was not paid to do so, but the British Show Jumping Association refused to rescind its decision.

That was not the end of Caroline's Olympic traumas. By 1980, the year of the Moscow Olympics, which were eventually boycotted by most of the western nations, she had been having great success on the big grey gelding Tigre, whom she owned jointly with Donald Bannocks. However, at the beginning of that year Mr Bannocks tried to sell Tigre 'because he wanted the horse to be ridden in the Olympics, and Caroline had turned professional by this time,' says Doreen Bradley. 'That was the start of all Caroline's problems over Tigre. Now you can see why we don't want to know about the Olympics.'

The Bradleys' decision on the Olympics was understood by John Whitaker, who had resigned himself to the fact that he would not be going to Seoul, but the selection committee found it harder to accept. General Sir Cecil Blacker, chairman of the selectors at that time, and Ronnie Massarella, the manager of the British team, did their best to persuade the Bradleys to change their minds. 'We felt it was the best opportunity we had ever had of winning an individual gold medal, and to have done so would have been the best thing for show jumping in Britain, which had a diminishing profile at the time,' explains General Blacker. Ronnie Massarella said at the time that Milton's absence would reduce Britain's chances of winning a medal by fifty per cent, so highly did he rate the horse.

Feelings were also running high among the riders. David Broome was quoted in *The Times* of June 7th that year pointing out that the British Federation had spent a lot of money allowing the horse to travel to international shows from which the Bradley's had benefited. At the Royal International Horse Show two weeks later an open letter was sent to Mr and Mrs Bradley from all the riders on

The Nations Cup meeting at Hickstead in 1988. Milton jumped the only double clear round for the British team on the same day that it was announced that he would definitely not be going to the Olympics. In this picture Milton is clearing a large oxer in the final round against the clock in the Grand Prix. 'It looks as if I've jumped the fence across from left to right,' explains John. 'Sometimes Milton can be a bit slow, but because I can turn shorter than most into a big fence like this, and probably turn quicker after, I save time. I can also jump a fence at more of an angle than I could risk with any other horse.'

the short-list for the Olympic Games, asking them to reconsider their decision. The letter said that, without Milton, 'we feel that our chances of winning may be catastrophically reduced. We realise that one of us will suffer if he takes part but, nevertheless, we feel that the success of the British team is vital.' No formal response was made to the letter, but it was clear that there was little hope of the Bradleys changing their minds over this emotive issue.

The press had a field day over the affair. 'It was unbelievable how bad the pressure was,' says Doreen Bradley. 'We came out of the house one day, after we had refused to talk to someone on the telephone, to find a cameraman standing outside the door. We were very upset by the whole thing. The vindictiveness was incredible, and we felt totally ostracised.'

For John Whitaker, the man in the middle of the row, it was a difficult time. 'I got the impression that the officials felt that I wasn't pushing the Bradleys hard enough to get them to let Milton go. But they had always said he couldn't. Of course I hoped that they might change their minds, but I think pushing them was the wrong way to go about it.'

The intensity of the campaign reached such a pitch that John very nearly lost his ride on the horse. Once it was known that Milton was not available for the Olympics, the BSJA did not want him to participate in any Nations Cup meetings, preferring instead to see the potential Olympic team horses perform in these competitions. The Bradleys were so annoyed by the decision that they almost sent Milton abroad, so that the horse could still take part in the Nations Cup meetings, albeit for a different country.

'The worst thing about it for me,' says John, 'was that I knew that Milton was at his peak (he is still just as good now, but he is not going to get any better), and with the Olympics coming only every four years it is difficult to get a horse at his best at the right time. I had had a similar disappointment with Ryan's Son. He was at his peak in 1980, when the Olympics should have been in Moscow. He came second at the 'Alternative Games' in Rotterdam, but it wasn't the same thing; then by the time we got to Los Angeles in 1984 he was past his best. I may never get another horse as good as Ryan's Son, let alone Milton, so I feel that the opportunity for me to win an individual Olympic medal has been lost.'

Nevertheless, John did not let the disappointment, or the hullabaloo that surrounded the affair, affect his performances with Milton. On the day the Bradleys gave their definitive answer to the question of Milton's availability for Seoul, the horse jumped the only double clear for the British team in the Nations Cup at Hickstead. Two weeks later at the Royal International Horse Show at Birmingham he won the Daily Mail Cup on the opening night, was runner-up in the King George V Gold Cup, and won the Grand Prix. The following month he won another Grand Prix in Zurich.

Without the Nations Cup meetings and the Olympics Milton was more or less grounded for the rest of the summer, so he came out again at the Horse of the Year Show in October, when he well and truly rubbed salt in the wounds of all those who had wanted him to go to Seoul by winning four of the five classes in which he was entered, and coming a close second to the German Olympic team gold medallist, Franke Sloothaak, in the Grand Prix. The points he gained gave him the Leading Show Jumper of the Year title as well.

One of the classes Milton won at Wembley was the International Masters, a new competition that year in which the winner takes all – £25,000 in this case. The seven qualifiers for the class have to jump a course of five fences, one of which is raised higher every time a rider jumps clear, and every time that happens the prize-money is increased by £1000. As each competitor enters the

Jumping the triple bar at Hickstead (1988) 'It is the sort of fence where Milton can really use his scope and power,' says John. 'You don't need to be quite so accurate at these fences, so I tend to ride him with more leg and give him more freedom, whereas at a vertical I would have to protect him a bit.'

arena he tells the steward which fence he would like put up, and he must then jump the course clear to stay in the competition.

If someone had been asked to design a class especially to suit Milton, they could not have done better. It is tailor-made for him. As the fences get bigger and the other horses begin to struggle, Milton comes into his own, and he has no difficulty in making the height (the planks stood at 6ft in the final round in 1988). Not surprisingly, he has won all the Masters competitions up until 1990.

Two weeks after achieving his record four wins and a second at Wembley, Milton won the Grand Prix in Stuttgart, his fourth Grand Prix victory of the year. He then won the World Cup qualifier in Bordeaux before going to Olympia, where his third place in the World Cup qualifier took him to the top of the European League. (While Milton was having a day's rest at Olympia, John flew to Grenoble to win £20,000 in the Grand Prix there on Gammon.) So Milton and John began the 1989 season heading the European League, and with their sights set on a World Cup victory.

*   *   *

In the run-up to the 1989 World Cup final Milton won the Grand Prix at the Dortmund show and the World Cup qualifier in Geneva. The final was held in April at Tampa, Florida, where a certain amount of friction developed between the Europeans and Americans over the quarantine restrictions: the European horses were confined to a concrete area next to the stables, whereas the Americans were allowed to ride their horses round the showground. 'I could understand the reason, in theory,' said John, 'but it didn't make much sense when we were mixing with the American horses in the collecting ring anyway. It was a bit annoying, but I don't think it really affected the results!'

It was Milton's third attempt at the World Cup final and, incidentally, John's tenth – he is the only rider to have competed in every final since the competition began in 1979. It looked this time as if John and Milton might at last achieve victory, but they were thwarted by the exceptionally consistent jumping of Ian Millar's Big Ben, who won all three rounds of the competition and had only one fence down throughout. This victory for the Canadian rider meant that he was the only person to have won the final in consecutive years, but he did not remain the sole record-holder for long. Within two years John, with the help of Milton, had equalled it.

However, in Tampa Milton had to settle for second place. He had jumped a good round against the clock, going clear and finishing in third place, but in the second leg he had a fence down in the first round and dropped to fifth place overall. He managed to pull back up again in the final competition by jumping two clear rounds; by this time, though, Millar was well out in front, and only a series of mistakes could have lost him the title.

At the 1989 World Cup final in Tampa the European horses were confined to a concrete area near the stables because of the quarantine regulations. Milton is probably wondering why he cannot be exercised somewhere more interesting.

Undeterred, John took Milton to Cannes in May and won the Grand Prix, and then on to Hickstead, where they were third in the Grand Prix and jumped two clear rounds for the British team in the Nations Cup, their last Nations Cup outing before the European Championships in Rotterdam in August.

The Royal International was not a great success that year because John, who was busy commuting between Birmingham and Germany so that he could compete in the Nations Cup meeting in Aachen with Gammon, kept losing out to his younger brother, Michael. When Milton had been in a strong position to win his first King George V Gold Cup after a reasonably fast clear against the clock in the final jump-off, Michael had then ridden such a speedy round on Didi that he finished 3 seconds under Milton's time. So once again, Milton was runner-up in this prestigious class. The following evening, John dashed back from

Milton making friends with the French horse Morgat at the World Cup final in Tampa, Florida, in 1989. 'He's a bit soft,' says John. 'He tends to get attached to horses he travels with, and then he gets upset when they leave him.'

competing, unsuccessfully, in the Grand Prix in Aachen, only to drop a fence with Milton in the first round of the Grand Prix at Birmingham. Michael was the victor in that class as well. One consolation for John was that Milton had won the opening international competition of the show, and, with less than two months to go before the European Championships, he was obviously still on form.

Just to prove this, Milton won the Grand Prix in Zurich three weeks later, and then jumped well at the Dubai Cup meeting at Hickstead and at the international show in Mondorf Le Bains before travelling to Rotterdam.

It was in Rotterdam that Milton finally laid claim to a championship title. He and John won the individual European gold medal, and the British team set a new record by winning a third successive gold medal in a European Championships. Added to that, Michael Whitaker took the silver individual medal, making it a family double. For John, this was the best moment in his career. He had come so close to gaining the individual title in the past (he had been second with Ryan's Son in 1983, third with Hopscotch in 1985, and second with Milton in 1987), that at times he had felt he was destined never actually to win it.

Hickstead Nations Cup, 1989, where Milton jumped a double clear for the British team.

It was a memorable occasion, too, for the Bradleys. In spite of suffering a horrendous car accident on the way home from Olympia the previous year, in which she was very nearly killed, Doreen Bradley had managed to travel to Rotterdam with her husband Tom to watch the championships. Their efforts were rewarded when Milton gained the individual title in the very same arena in which Caroline had helped the British team to win a gold medal ten years earlier.

John Whitaker

'Sometimes I get so carried away on Milton I ask him to do something that is almost impossible, but he's so good he manages it. Then I try it on another horse and I find myself upside down.'

Although the British victory looked relatively easy on paper – they finished 13.06 points ahead of France – it was a closely fought contest both for the team and individual titles. Things had started well for Milton, who, for the first time in a championship or World Cup final, actually won the speed class on the first day. The course, designed by Olaf Petersen, had suited Milton well, for it was big but with no awkward turns or dog-legs into the fences. 'It was our kind of course,' said John afterwards. 'Milton got better the further he went.'

The other riders on the British team – Michael Whitaker (Monsanta), Nick Skelton (Apollo) and Joe Turi (Kruger) – all faulted, but Nick and Michael went fast enough to finish on good scores. There is an incomprehensible system at these championships that converts time faults to penalties, which when computed put Britain 1.06 points ahead of France, with Holland only a further 1.55 points away. The individual placings were also close, with less than three points separating the top four places, although one of the favourites, Pierre Durand with Jappeloup, who won the European title in St Gallen and the individual gold medal in Seoul, had gone out of contention after a complete miss at the sixth fence, which they had crashed through.

Nick Skelton

'I don't think we've ever seen his equal. In a big, outdoor arena he is perhaps beatable, but in a competition where consistent jumping is needed there's no other horse that can live with him. His greatest asset is his consistency. In Nations Cup competitions it is always good to know that you have a reliable back-up coming at the end. The European Championships in Rotterdam was the best competition that I have seen him win. The last round was very big, but he just played with the fences. He has a foot start over every other horse.'

John with his brother Michael during the Nations Cup parade at Hickstead, 1989.

Milton getting excited during the prize-giving at the 1989 European Championships in Rotterdam, where he and John won the individual and team gold medals. 'I went through a phase of putting running-reins on him during the presentations because he got so strong,' says John.

For the second leg of the championship, the Nations Cup, which decides the team medals, Britain was drawn seventh of the thirteen nations competing and began to dominate proceedings when the team's first three riders, Nick, Michael and Joe, all jumped clear in the first round. Since it is the scores of the best three in each round that count towards the final result, in a normal Nations Cup, Milton, the last to go for the British team, need not have jumped in this round; however, as in St Gallen two years earlier, he had to complete the course to establish his individual position. But this time Milton had a fence down. It was an upright near the area where the competitors stand. 'There was no apparent reason for it,' said John. 'It was just one of those things.'

Fortunately, it did not have a significant effect on the individual placings, as most of the other serious contenders also made mistakes, but when Milton had a foot in the water in the second round, John began to grow despondent. 'I felt that the individual title was slipping away,' he says. 'Milton had had a silly fence down in the first round, and then when he put a foot in the water – which he never does – I just thought that things weren't going to work out for him.' As it turned out, John had not lost too much ground, and he was still lying second in the individual placings before the final competition. However, his brother Michael, by virtue of his double clear in the Nations Cup (he was the only rider in Rotterdam to achieve this), had moved up into first place, just over 3 points ahead of John.

Joe Turi

'Milton is without doubt the greatest show jumper I have ever seen. His most remarkable quality is his consistency. Added to that is his amazing scope, superb temperament and phenomenal athleticism. Being grey helps to create more of a spectacle when he jumps – he surely should have been named Pegasus.

He definitely enjoys all the attention he receives; he is a real showman. He has a disconcerting habit of blowing raspberries when you have your back to him!

His record in Nations Cup competitions is of clear round after clear round. To have him on your side is a real psychological advantage. Of all the times I have seen him compete, the one that sticks in my mind is his winning round in the first leg of the European Championships in Rotterdam, which was a speed class. He won it the most outstanding manner. I don't think there has ever been a horse that could have beaten him that day.'

With the team gold secure, the two brothers prepared to do battle for individual honours. In the final competition both John and Michael achieved clears in the first round, and although Michael collected half a time fault he remained in the lead. John then kept the pressure on Michael by jumping another clear on Milton, who was not making any mistakes this time, and then he had to sit and watch what happened to his brother.

'It was very difficult watching Michael, because I didn't want to wish him a fence down, but at the same time I knew that if he did have one down I would win.' When Michael did make that one fateful error, John did not know whether to laugh or cry. 'I had such mixed feelings: disappointment for Michael, but of course I was pleased to have won. It wasn't quite the same as beating a foreigner though.' It was nonetheless a great victory for John and Milton – their first individual championship title – and a just reward for missing out on the chance of an Olympic medal a year earlier.

> **Michael Whitaker**
>
> *'The best things about Milton are that he's got a lot of scope – more scope than anything else – and he's very easy to train. He always listens and he's basically very careful. He also has a fantastic temperament. At the shows he's always happy and he has the right attitude for the job.*
>
> *When I had a fence down in the last round at the European Championships in Rotterdam I was disappointed for myself of course, but at least it meant that John had won. I was very happy for him. He was thirty-four then and hadn't won a major championship, and at the time I think he really needed that victory.'*

The dual victory by the two brothers could not have been better timed. Only weeks before the European Championships they had learnt that their sponsor, Next, was withdrawing its support at the end of the year. After their performance in Rotterdam, it did not seem likely that the Whitakers would have any trouble in securing a new sponsor, and sure enough a contract was soon drawn up with Henderson Unit Trust Management. The deal did not please the Bradleys, however, because they did not like the idea of their horse being called Henderson Milton. 'We weren't consulted about it,' says Mrs Bradley, 'but in the end we had to accept it because we didn't really want to take the horse away from John.' So at the end of that year Next Milton became Henderson Milton.

After the European Championships the season was by no means over for Milton. A trip to Calgary at the beginning of September was followed by Bremen, in Germany, before the Horse of the Year Show at Wembley, where Milton won the opening class as well as the valuable Masters competition, this time collecting £27,000 in prize-money. 'Marvellous Milton is Master – again' read the title to the *Horse and Hound* report of the show, which referred to Milton as 'show jumping's wonder horse'. By now the big grey gelding with the extravagant action had won the hearts of show jumping fans both in this country and abroad, and whenever he entered an arena he would be greeted by thunderous applause and cheers from the spectators.

Three weeks later he was in Stuttgart winning another car, this time a Mercedes (Milton had already won six Volvos in World Cup competitions during his career), then on to Vienna (third in the Grand Prix and first in another class), Maastricht and Bordeaux before winning the Grand Prix in Frankfurt at the beginning of December. But he had to settle for second place behind Franke Sloothaak and Walzerkoenig (whom he had relegated to the runner-up position in Frankfurt) in the Grand Prix at Olympia.

Milton's successes that autumn had helped to bring his prize-money total for 1989 up to £206,729, a record for a British horse. On that basis alone, it had been an outstanding year, but for John it was the European Championship victory that stood out above all else.

Lap of honour time at the 1989 European Championships in Rotterdam. 'Winning the championships was a mixture of relief and delight,' says John. 'I was so pleased to have won and not come second again. I was beginning to think I would never do it.'

51

Milton jumping the second part of the double of water ditches in Calgary, 1989. It was a fence that caused quite a few problems because it was very big and sited near the collecting ring. John explains the sequence:

(a) 'I still have quite a bit of contact as Milton prepares to take off. I was committed to my stride at this stage because the fence was the second part of a double.'

(c) 'Giving him his freedom over the fence.'

(b) 'My job is done now and there is nothing else I can do to help him except to release his head and go with him.'

(d) 'He has not quite landed, but I have started to sit up and look for the next fence.'

4.

Higher and Higher

Milton made an auspicious start to 1990 by winning at least one class at each of his four international outings before the World Cup final in April. Antwerp was the first of these, followed by Paris, where he won the World Cup qualifier; then S'Hertogenbosch (first in the World Cup qualifier and winner of another class) and finally Gothenburg, where he won the Grand Prix. Unlike 1988, however, this time he had not peaked too soon, and in Dortmund, two weeks later, John became the first British rider ever to win the World Cup final – and only the second European rider to win it since the tournament began in 1979.

Milton says hello to Doreen Bradley, while exercising in S'Hertogenbosch, 1990.

Milton arriving in Stockholm to compete in the World Championships, 1990. 'He travels very well,' says John. 'He eats and sleeps normally when he gets to shows and doesn't fret. He can sometimes hold up a plane by ten or fifteen minutes, though, because he doesn't want to go on. He hangs about and has a good look round, and then, when he's made up his mind to go, he just walks straight up the ramp.'

Milton doing his Spanish Riding School act after wining the Grand Prix in Gothenburg, 1990.

For the last ten years the North Americans had dominated the final, with riders from the USA winning it seven times and Canadians three times, so the German crowd was delighted to see the trophy go to a European, especially as the winner was their favourite horse. Milton had jumped superbly throughout the competition; the only fence he had down was in the final round of the third leg, and by then he already had three fences in hand over the runner-up, Pierre Durand and Jappeloup.

John and Milton had won the first leg (the speed class) by just 0.20 seconds from Pierre and Jappeloup, and had then come a close second to Nick Skelton and Grand Slam in the next leg, so they were well placed going into the final competition. There were, however, some good combinations not far behind, including Franke Sloothaak with Walzerkoenig, Jan Tops with Doreen la Silla, and, of course, Pierre Durand with Jappeloup.

For the final leg of the competition the course designer, Olaf Petersen, had designed an extraordinarily diverse course for the small, indoor arena. There was an ornamental lake, a water jump and a double of ditches, all intended to be 'pleasing to the eye for the public'. But many riders felt he had gone a bit over the top, especially as the long, thirteen-fence course had some exceptionally big obstacles with complicated distances.

Pierre Durand

'When in action, Milton is, in my opinion, the very expression of grace and agility. I often compare him with a feather that would draw arabesques above fences.

As an outside observer I have the feeling that, besides his outstanding jumping abilities, Milton owns a character of rare stability and quietness, which is an upmost asset at the highest level in show jumping.

Facing Milton [in a competition] always means having to surpass oneself. Thanks to him I succeeded with Jappeloup in going beyond my limits in many circumstances, especially during our famous "mano à mano" at the European Championships in St Gallen in 1989.

Milton and Jappeloup are totally opposite, and not only because of their coats, but these two star horses have often succeeded during their duels in provoking rare emotions and in raising our sport to an artistic level.'

In the second round he created a double of water-tray ditches on a curve, so that the horses had to turn as they jumped the two fences. 'It was a bit gimmicky really, especially for indoors,' said John. 'In the second round things were taken to the extreme in terms of size and difficulty, and I felt it wasn't fair on the horses. Even Milton was struggling over the last line, and when he had a rail down I was very disappointed, even though I knew we'd won. He had tried so hard, he didn't deserve a fence down.

'Normally I prefer the courses to be big, because that suits Milton. When the other riders are complaining about the size, I'll be the one to stand back and say nothing. But with the type of fences they were using in Dortmund, especially after three hard days of competition, I think it was too much. You shouldn't have to push horses to the limit to get results.'

Nevertheless Milton had proved that even the toughest of courses were not a problem for him, and the World Cup final had certainly not dampened his enthusiasm for jumping. At Hickstead two months later he was second in the Grand Prix and had a double clear in the Nations Cup; then at the Royal International Horse Show in Birmingham, he finally put paid to his 'second place' jinx in the King George V Gold Cup, which he won after achieving the only clear round in the final jump-off. 'It meant a lot to me to win that competition,' said John. 'It is a very old and prestigious class, and Milton had been unlucky not to win it before.' He had been third in 1987, and second in both 1988 and 1989.

On the same day as Milton won the King George V Gold Cup, Emma-Jane

Brown won the ladies' equivalent, the Queen Elizabeth II Cup, which gave an added emotional significance to the occasion. Emma-Jane had started her competitive career with Caroline Bradley, and Caroline had won the Queen's Cup in 1978 on Milton's sire, Marius.

Milton had now won nearly every major title – except the World Championships. This was the next big event on his calendar, and preparations for Stockholm began soon after the Royal International. Milton, together with the rest of the British team, competed in Franconville, Zurich and Luxembourg, the latter two shows having Fibresand arenas so that the horses could accustom themselves to competing on this man-made surface, which many riders feel is not as satisfactory as real grass or the soil used at indoor shows.

Competing at Hickstead in 1990, where Milton jumped a double clear in the Nations Cup (his third successive double clear at Hickstead). Even Milton is having to stretch over this large oxer to make sure that he clears it. 'When he needs that little bit more, he can usually find it,' says John.

Cantering past the famous Hickstead Bank, which Milton has never been down.

Emma-Jane Brown

'I remember Milton from the time I was working at Caroline Bradley's yard, where I learnt the basics about schooling young horses. He was a lovely novice who enjoyed his jumping even then, and he was always friendly in the stable.

I think John and Milton are a remarkable pair. It's a one-off thing that such a brilliant horse and rider should have come together.'

59

Exercising in Franconville, France, where Milton came second in the Grand Prix, only a month before the World Championships in Stockholm, 1990.

The championships for the show jumping were part of the World Equestrian Games in Stockholm, a new venture that brought all the equestrian disciplines – dressage, three-day eventing, show-jumping, vaulting, driving and endurance riding – to one venue for their respective World Championships. It was a brilliant concept, enjoyed by riders and spectators, and most people were impressed by how well it was organised. In terms of publicity it was an outstanding success, as every discipline had the world's equestrian media focussed upon it. However, this unprecedented attention nearly backfired when allegations of cruelty to show jumpers were released to coincide with the Games.

The allegations came after a film was broadcast on television showing the German rider and trainer, Paul Schockemöhle, rapping horses (i.e. hitting a horse on the legs with a stick to make it jump higher), and there was a great hullabaloo in the press about it. However, once the show jumping was underway the affair was soon forgotten, and the German team, even without its top rider Franke Sloothaak, who had withdrawn from the Games as a result of the allegations (he is one of Paul Schockemöhle's pupils), gained the silver medal.

Jumping in the speed competition, the first leg of the World Championships in Stockholm, 1990. The planks were curved so John has tried to pick out the lowest point, and as they come down he is getting ready to turn left-handed.

Clearing the ducks in the warm-up class, Stockholm, 1990. Although Milton is quite a spookey horse he does not usually worry about strange-looking fences. If anything, they make him more aware of the fence and therefore more likely to clear it.

Stockholm was a disappointment for the British show jumpers. The team, with its impressive European Championship record, started out as one of the favourites, but luck was not on its side. One thing that was never in any doubt, though, was Milton's popularity. Some of his fans had made a huge banner proclaiming 'WE LOVE MILTON', and he was greeted like a pop star every time he came into the arena. The atmosphere was tremendous, and Milton revelled in it, but at times his attention was obviously diverted, costing him faults.

Milton does not often wear a fringe, but it was hot in Stockholm and he was bothered by the flies.

Jumping at his best. At times Milton was distracted by the spectators in Stockholm, who greeted him like a pop star every time he came into the arena.

David Broome

'The first time I came across Milton was at Newark Show, and after I'd seen him jumping I asked Caroline [Bradley] how much she wanted for him. She said he wasn't for sale. When I persisted she eventually said to me: 'I really don't want to sell him because I think this one is good enough for the Olympics.' She agreed to let me have first chance if she ever changed her mind about selling him. I think Caroline's dream was to ride that horse at the Olympics, but six weeks later she was dead.

The next time I saw Milton was at Park Farm, when Steve Hadley had him. I watched him jumping the combination there one evening in a class that I wasn't even riding in, and I remember thinking to myself that if there was ever a horse worth £100,000 it's him. It's nice to find that your judgment isn't totally out.'

In the initial speed competition all four of the British team horses faulted, and the team finished in sixth place – not a very encouraging start. Then in the first round of the Nations Cup Michael Whitaker was the only rider on the British team to go clear; the others, including John and Milton, all made mistakes. 'I think Milton was distracted,' said John, who had one fence down. 'We jumped the combination on the far side of the arena, and the crowd cheered. Then all the cameramen ran along the side of the arena so that they could take another picture of Milton as we jumped the gate. There was a bit of a dog-leg to the gate, and I don't think he saw the fence properly because he was too busy watching the cameramen. He hit it half way up. Normally, if he does have a fence down, he just touches it, but he smashed the gate in Stockholm.'

Fortunately his next round was clear, but both David Broome and Nick Skelton continued to have unlucky faults. 'Everyone was jumping well,' said John. 'It was just that we all had some silly fences down. In a competition of this sort it is better to have one person having all the faults, and the others jumping clear; you don't want the mistakes spread about as they were with us.' However, Michael pulled off another clear with Monsanta (collecting just 0.25 of a time penalty) to bring the British team into the bronze medal position behind France and Germany.

Although the British riders felt they could have done better, there was consolation when John and Milton qualified for the final individual competition, in which the top four competitors ride each other's horses as well as their own.

Penny Stevens, Milton's groom, leading Milton between rounds in the final leg of the World Championships in Stockholm. The four riders are allowed to use their own saddles on the other horses.

Greg Best (USA), the first of the four finalists to ride Milton. 'I don't think Greg realised how much leg I use on Milton,' says John. 'His own horse, Gem Twist, is much sharper and tends to pull you into the fence. I think Greg sat too still on Milton, which is why he had those two fences down at the combination. The other riders got the benefit of Greg's mistake, because Milton only had one more fence down after that. I think the French riders preferred Milton to Gem Twist because Milton does as he is told, so you are in control all the time, whereas Gem Twist likes to do things his own way.'

John was thrilled. 'It had been my ambition to get into the last four in the World Championships. I always felt that if I could get into that position I could do quite well because I am used to riding a lot of different horses.' Milton, on the other hand, had not been jumped by anyone but John for over six years.

After completing one round over the big, but fairly straightforward course, each of the finalists was allowed three minutes in a railed-off section of the arena to warm up on their next horse. Milton had gone clear for John, and next it was the American, Greg Best's turn to ride him. Greg was in awe of Milton, and he found the contrast between him and his own grey horse, Gem Twist, who is very quick and sharp, considerable. 'With Gem Twist, you can just sit there and let him get on with it, whereas with Milton you have to use quite a bit of leg as he leaves the ground to give him enough impetus,' says John. 'I don't think Greg Best appreciated quite how much leg I do ride him with, and he took Milton into the combination a bit too casually.' That cost the American 8 faults, but he came back to the warm-up area more concerned that he had upset Milton than by the fact that he had incurred penalties.

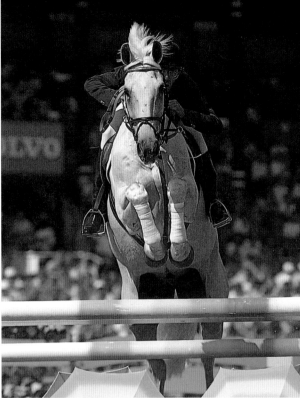

Above left: *The French rider Eric Navet riding Milton in the final competition when the four competitors ride each other's horses. It was the first time that Milton had jumped with another rider for over six years, but he went clear for Eric Navet, helping him to win the individual gold medal.*

Above right: *Frenchman Hubert Bourdy riding Milton in the final competition of the World Championships in Stockholm, 1990. They had one fence down.*

John's second ride was on the French horse Morgat (Hubert Bourdy), and it was in this round, in which he collected 8 faults, that the prospects of a gold medal begin to diminish. 'Morgat was the one horse that I thought I could probably ride well because he is quite a small, sharp horse, and you need to be accurate with him. I think I am better suited to that kind of horse. (Milton is the opposite: I have had to learn to adapt to him.) But I underestimated Morgat's ability. I thought he would find it difficult to make the width of the big combination, so I over-rode him at it, sending him in a bit long and flat, instead of getting close to it. That round on Morgat blew the gold medal for me.'

Milton, unaware that he was helping the opposition, then jumped an excellent clear round for the Frenchman Eric Navet, collecting half a time fault, before having one fence down with his final rider, Hubert Bourdy. The changes in jockey had not concerned him at all, and he had jumped as well as he could for his new riders. John, meanwhile, had a fence down with Malesan Quito de Baussy (Eric Navet's horse) and a clear round on Gem Twist to take the individual silver medal behind Eric Navet.

> **Eric Navet**
> Comments after riding Milton in the World Championships in Stockholm:
> 'He was fantastic. I didn't think it was possible for a horse to jump like that.
> It was an honour to ride him.'

> **Greg Best**
> Comments after riding Milton in the World Championships in Stockholm:
> 'I should have ridden him more aggressively. For me the thought of riding
> Milton was like being told you'd got a date with the most beautiful girl in the
> world – you find yourself tripping over your feet.'

'I was quite pleased to have finished second,' says John. 'And I enjoyed the competition. It was interesting jumping the other horses. You set off trying to ride them in the same way as their own riders, but by the time you have jumped a couple of fences you revert back to your own style because you are too busy concentrating on trying to clear the fences to worry about the way you are riding. I don't totally agree with the system for finding the World Champion. It makes an exciting competition for the spectators, but doesn't give a true result because there is too much emphasis on the rider. It should be the combination that wins. That's what show jumping is all about – the horse and rider.'

*   *   *

At Wembley the following October John and Milton won the Masters competition for the third consecutive year, though they very nearly missed their chance to compete in it by failing to qualify. There had been three classes in which horses could qualify for the Masters. In the first, the Pedigree Chum Classic, Milton had a refusal, which is almost unheard of for him. 'Everyone thought it was a major catastrophe,' recalled John, 'but it didn't worry me in the slightest. It was just a misunderstanding.' In the subsequent qualifier, the Modern Alarms Cup, they missed their chance again by failing, by a mere 0.28 seconds, to finish in the top two. Their last opportunity to qualify came in a speed class just a few hours before the Masters, but Milton was 0.28 seconds too slow again, allowing Nigel Coupe's Invincible Lad to snatch third place from them (the top three qualified). As luck would have it, though, Nigel then opted to withdraw from the Masters, so Milton took his place.

'The speed competition had been a good class in its own right,' explained John, 'so Nigel had gone in for it even though he didn't particularly want to qualify for the Masters. Anyway, Michael [Whitaker], who trains Nigel, told him

HRH The Princess Royal talks to Milton after presenting the individual show jumping awards on the final day of the World Equestrian Games. John had narrowly missed winning the gold medal.

that he wouldn't have a chance of winning the Masters, and convinced him to pull out.' John and Milton duly won £29,000 in prize-money, much to the chagrin of the other competitors, and the following day came a close second to Nick Skelton and Grand Slam in the Grand Prix.

After Wembley came Stuttgart, usually a good show for Milton, but this year things did not go according to plan. In the class for the Mercedes, which they had won the previous year, John and Milton collected a time fault in the first round, putting them out of contention. John was not pleased with himself for that mistake. Determined to make amends in the Grand Prix, he was going all out for a fast clear in the final jump-off when disaster struck: he fell off.

The course for the jump-off against the clock was very twisty, and there was one particular fence where the horses had to turn right immediately on landing, whereas in the two previous rounds they had turned left. John came into the arena knowing that Jos Lansink had already achieved a fast clear round, so he turned very sharply into this fence to save time. Milton screwed a bit over it and half unseated John, who found himself leaning out to the right as they landed. Unaccustomed to finding his jockey hanging round his neck, Milton panicked slightly and jinxed to the left – which was the way he thought he should be going anyway – and John went off to the right. 'It felt as if it was all happening in slow motion,' said John. 'Milton went one way and I went the other.'

Up to that point he had been faster than Jos, and he had only one fence left to jump. Doreen Bradley, who was watching the class recalls: 'It was such a funny thing. When it happened, Milton turned round to look at John as if to say, "What did you go that way for?" He had such a comical expression on his face.'

Harvey Smith

'Milton is the best show jumper there has ever been. When it comes to consistency, that one takes the biscuit. He never seems to have a bad day. He's always the same.

It is his temperament that makes him so good. The only thing he wants to do is jump, so he is never looking for a way out. The greatest thing in Milton's favour, though, is that he found John. Those two are spot on. They suit each other so well.

There has never been a horse like Milton. The one that comes closest to him is Ted Williams' Pegasus, who was the leading show jumper in Britain during the 1950s. He had the same quality of lightness; if you shut your eyes when Milton is jumping you can't hear him. He is like a ballerina; he is so light on his feet.'

Winners of the 1991 World Cup final for the second successive year: John and Milton acknowledge the tumultuous applause from the crowd in the Gothenburg stadium.

71

After Stuttgart came Vienna and then Maastricht, and the plan after that was to take Milton to Hanover where he would rest for a few days before going to Frankfurt. But while in Hanover Milton developed a slight temperature and, worse still, went off his food. 'That's pretty serious for him,' says John. So he was taken straight back to his own stable at home. Once there, however, his condition deteriorated: he did not eat, and just stood in his box with his head down. Much to everyone's relief he began to pick up again after a few days, but by then it was too late to get him ready for Olympia, so Milton began his winter break a little earlier than usual. It was the first time in his six years with John that he had had an illness or injury that had prevented him from competing.

*   *   *

At the beginning of 1991 John began working Milton sooner than usual because the horse had already had a long rest after his illness. A week of walking was followed by a gradual increase in work, until, after about five weeks, he was ready for his first show of the season. He had an outing in February at the South View Equestrian Centre, where he won his class, before going on to S'Hertogenbosch to finish second in the World Cup qualifier. In Dortmund the following week he was fourth in the qualifier and first in another class, and in Paris a week later he was fourth again in the World Cup qualifier. Then he came home for a couple of weeks' rest before the long trip to Gothenburg for the final.

John had decided to take Milton to Gothenburg by a rather long and complicated route because he was anxious to avoid the twenty-four-hour boat crossing from Harwich to Gothenburg. 'It is quite a risk going on such a long boat trip with horses,' explains John. 'If they become ill half way across there is nothing you can do to help them. You can't change the temperature, or get them out of the box and walk them around. You are stuck there. At least if you are on the road you can stop and find a stable for them somewhere.'

So Milton took four days to reach Gothenburg. He set off in his box from West Yorkshire with the two other horses accompanying him on the trip, Gammon and Fonda, for the drive to Harwich, spending the night there before taking the boat to the Hook of Holland, where he again stayed overnight. The following day there was a drive to Hamburg and a third overnight stop, and then on to Gothenburg by boat the next morning. Although the journey had taken a lot of organisation, John felt it was worth the trouble: Milton arrived the day before the show began, in excellent form, and John was able to ride him that afternoon.

Unfortunately the draw for the speed competition, the first leg of the final, was not a good one for John. He was drawn to go fourth out of forty-four, which meant that he would have no yardstick by which to judge his pace; most of the good horses and riders would be jumping after him. 'I'll just have to do my own thing,' he said at the time, which meant going as fast as he could without taking too many risks. He steadied slightly for the more difficult fences, a double of planks and another of square oxers, but took a calculated flier on the long gallop to the triple bar to finish clear in 60.48 seconds. Only two riders improved on his score – Otto Becker with Pamina, who got round in 58.13 seconds, and Franke Sloothaak on Walzerkoenig who were fractionally slower. So John finished the first leg in third place, a position with which, considering the draw, he was reasonably satisfied.

The next day Milton was 'jumping out of his skin', according to John, but he had one of those unlucky knock-downs that could easily have cost him the trophy: he just nudged a brick on the wall with his front feet, and although it did not fall down at that point, Milton flicked it off with his back legs as he was landing. 'I thought, "oh well, that's blown it again,"' said John, but, amazingly, every single rider in the top thirteen overnight places faulted in the first round of the second leg, so John and Milton were able to retain their third place.

In fact their mistake could have been a blessing in disguise, because it meant that Milton missed the two jump-offs in the second leg and had freshness on his side for the final class. It pleased John that the courses, designed by Roland Nilsson, who had stepped in at the last minute when ill-health had prevented Philippe Gayot from doing the job, were not as demanding as the track in Dortmund the previous year. However, there were some difficult distance problems to be tackled, especially in the final leg.

Fortunately, Milton's jumping that day was in a class of its own. His first clear round brought him up into second place when Pamina made a mistake, and his second clear – the only double clear achieved that day – left no room for error for the leaders, Nelson Pessoa with Special Envoy. When the Brazilian had a fence down, Milton became the winner, and the packed stadium at Gothenburg erupted with cheers and applause.

Genevieve Murphy wrote in *The Independent* the following day: 'It is just

---

Nelson Pessoa

'I have only known Milton since he became the great international horse he is today – the best – and I must say that the complicity of the horse-rider combination is absolutely marvellous.

On his side, Milton has all the necessary qualities to be the champion he is: careful, brave, daring, agile and sound. On the other side, John's science as a rider and a horseman conducts Milton's career management perfectly.

To me, it is simply the strongest horse and rider combination of all time in show jumping history.'

***Judith Draper – Equestrian Correspondent,* The Daily Mail**

'In five unprecedented seasons as Britain's leading show jumper, Milton has become the answer to a journalist's prayers. Where he goes you can be sure of a story. Mention his name and even the most unhorsy of sports editors are inclined to take notice. Some may even be persuaded to allocate an extra line or two of space to a sport which is all too often squeezed out by football, cricket, golf or tennis.

The only problem for those writing about him on a regular basis lies in finding enough superlatives to describe his brilliance and consistency.

During twelve years as an equestrian writer, and many more as a follower of international show jumping, I can recall no horse who has commanded such universal adulation. Indeed, his banner-waving, bouquet-throwing fans at shows such as Gothenburg, Stuttgart and Paris are more numerous and vociferous than those at home. After his World Cup win is Gothenburg in 1991, photographs of Milton appeared on the front page of every Swedish daily newspaper.

And it is not only the public which is awestruck. Those who compete against him are equally filled with admiration. As Nelson Pessoa said after finishing runner-up to him in the 1991 World Cup final, "To be second to Milton is like winning."

Style, charisma, panache, good looks, he has them all. It is an honour to watch him jump – an even greater privilege to be paid to do so.'

as well that Milton, the idol of the capacity crowds here, relishes such attention. He was singled out for the noisiest adulation each time he entered the arena and, show-off that he is, he responded with a brilliant exhibition of powerful, precise jumping.' John and Milton were showered in flowers from the spectators after their second clear round, and everyone stayed for the prize-giving when John threw flowers from his bouquet back into the stands, to more rapturous applause. Milton then gave a lap of honour, ending with a performance of his special party piece – a dramatic leap into the air that would not look out of place in the Spanish Riding School.

It had been an exciting final that had kept everyone on the edge of their seats until near the end. Ronnie Massarella, the British team manager, had travelled to Gothenburg to watch the competition, even though he had barely recovered from three months of illness, during which time he had had

Hickstead, 1991, where Milton won the Grand Prix and jumped his fourth consecutive double clear in the Nations Cup.

A treat for Milton after the World Cup qualifier in Paris, 1991. Milton had spotted the tray of carrots as soon as it was carried into the arena, and his eyes never left it.

pneumonia, pleurisy and then a sinus operation. His journey had proved worthwhile. 'I thought I was going to have a heart attack!' he joked after watching the closing stages of the competition.

Milton had now gained another place in the record books as one of only two horses to have won the World Cup final in consecutive years, and he had also confirmed beyond any doubt that, among the top international show jumpers, he is the one who has captured the imagination and hearts of spectators throughout the world.

Ronnie Massarella – Manager of the British team

'I personally believe that Milton is the greatest show jumper the world has ever seen. He's like a machine. He has the power, the grace and the brains, and he loves the job – and that's essential.

If you look at the number of clear rounds he jumps and the number of competitions he wins, it's tremendous. Added to that he's grey, he's photogenic, he has a good outlook on life and the personality to go with it, and he has tremendous presence. I have never known a horse to be so popular. When he comes into the ring he is like a pop star entering the arena. The people adore him.

I am used to watching show jumping all the time and looking at a lot of horses, and having the pressure of my team horses, but Milton just seems special. I never expect him to knock a fence down, though of course he does occasionally, but it thrills me the way he goes about his job. Show jumping courses today are bigger and more technical than they have ever been, and Milton copes with them all terrifically well. It inspires confidence in me when I see him go into the ring, and the team riders know that if they have got John and Milton following them at number four they can rely on him to go well. It helps them to ride that extra per cent better because they have more confidence.

If you have Milton on your team at one of the Nations Cup meetings the whole team seems to bubble. That has a lot to do with John as well, because he is such a tremendous team member. He has a wonderful sense of humour, in his dry Yorkshire way, and he helps to create the spirit that you need with a good team. He's also a brilliant rider. Very cool and professional. He's got exceptionally good hands and, although he looks rather frail, he's actually a very strong rider and uses tremendous leg pressure, so the horse responds well.

I don't think Milton would have gone so well for any other rider. He has got the ability regardless of who rides him, but a lot of horses don't use their ability to the full because they just don't feel like it. John's attitude seems to suit the horse. His takes the approach: "Come on, boy, let's go and do it," but not in a flamboyant way; he's got a quiet style. He and Milton have similar characters. I think they're the greatest combination we are ever likely to see. We've been privileged to witness them over the last few years.'

5.

Milton at Home and Abroad

By all accounts Milton is a bit of a lunatic at home – particularly when he is taken out exercising. 'He'll spook at anything,' says John, 'and the trouble is he doesn't just look at the thing, he'll jump six feet in the air and then do the splits when he comes down again. He's like a small child who is so busy peering at something that he doesn't look where he is going. One day he shied away from an empty crisp bag and fell into a ditch. I had to climb off and lead him out, and he was covered in mud all down one side.'

Because of his uncontainable high spirits only John and his second rider, Tracey Newman, ever take Milton out on exercise. The responsibility can weigh heavily: 'He's a hairbrain on the roads,' says Tracey. 'I always take him out in knee-pads, and usually put on exercise bandages, as we are still wary of his split tendon operation. It has never given him any trouble, but we've always kept an eye on it. We do a lot of road work with him to keep him fit, but he's such a liability; I'm always worried that he'll come down on his knees. He trips up quite a bit anyway when he's walking along. I think he just doesn't pay attention and he's quite lazy with his feet.'

If it is very windy Tracey will not risk taking him on the roads, and instead exercises him in the school, but she never jumps him. Her objective is to keep him fit between shows, which in the Yorkshire Dales is not a problem; the horses at Heyside Farm have to climb a substantial hill just to get from the stableyard to the road.

Some horses need to be slightly less fit to give their best performance, otherwise they become too difficult to control, but Milton goes better the fitter he is. He is ridden up and down the hills at home and, when the weather is reasonable, taken for gallops once or twice a week. He jumps at home only when he has had a long rest and needs a quick reminder of what the job is all about; otherwise his jumping is confined to the shows. 'He's such an easy horse to prepare,' says John. 'I've never had any problems with him.'

When Milton is resting he is turned out during the day, but he has to be put in a field without much grass because he is incurably greedy and, given the opportunity, gets very fat in no time at all. He has a wood shavings bed in his stable, otherwise he would eat all the straw, and he frequently has to go on diets, which make him grumpy.

John likes to exercise Milton on the roads and moors as much as possible to keep him fit and prevent him getting bored, but he is a bit of a liability out hacking. 'He's so gormless when you're riding him out,' says John. 'He's just like a big kid. He'll look at something and walk into something else. He reminds me of 'Bambi on Ice'; he'll see a bird or a plastic bag and leap into the air. You just have to hope he doesn't do the splits when he comes down again.'

Anyone for a game of football? Milton taking time off at home in West Yorkshire. When he is not working he has a tendency to put on weight very quickly because he is so greedy.

'A lot of people probably think he is too fat when he is jumping,' says John, 'but he seems to be better for carrying a bit of weight; he has more energy. I tried getting him slimmer once as I thought it might help him to jump even better, but it didn't suit him. We've experimented with him a bit over the years, and I think we've got it about right now.'

When Milton goes in the field he is usually turned out on his own. John likes to keep the horses separate so that they don't kick each other, but Hopscotch often jumps into Milton's paddock to keep him company; and sometimes if the weather is bad, one of the children's ponies is turned out with him, otherwise Milton, who is a bit of a softy, will hang around by the gate in the hope that someone will take pity on him and take him back to his warm stable.

For a horse who has a fairly relaxed outlook on life, Milton has a surprising number of phobias. One of these is a fear of wires and hose-pipes, the sight of which will set the springs in his legs going. For this reason the series of electric fences around the fields at Heyside Farm, put up mainly to prevent the young horses leaning over the top of the rails, has to be switched off whenever Milton is turned out. 'I think that if he touched the electric fence when it was on, he'd be frightened to death and we'd never get near him again,' says Penny Stevens, his groom for the last five years.

Coming down the steep drive at Heyside Farm, the Whitakers' home.

80

At home with the family. Milton stands in front of the Whitakers' house, Heyside Farm, in West Yorkshire, with (left to right), Mindy (the dog), Robert, Clare, Joanne, Louise and John.

He is also neurotic about being clipped. He has always been very bad about it, which is why he injured himself at Steve Hadley's yard, and even now John has to dope him before he is clipped. 'We try to give him a little less tranquilliser each time, so that he might gradually get over it, but he doesn't seem to get any better. It's something we've just had to accept, and we try to clip him as little as possible. He's always been quite sensitive about having his girths done up and things like that. He'll nip you and then make a run for it.'

Pulling his tail is also a major performance. John's wife Clare has to stand outside the stable on a crate with Milton's tail over the top of the stable door and pull it from there, while John has him twitched at the front end. 'Otherwise he'd kick you from here to Barnsley,' says Penny.

Milton in the mud. 'He's probably thinking he should be inside where it's nice and warm,' says John. 'We try to treat him like a normal horse. You can't wrap him up in cotton wool.'

Milton accompanied by his miniature replica, Bo-bo, Joanne's Shetland pony. John often rides with his children, and the two eldest are already keen on jumping.

All in all Milton keeps the Whitaker establishment on its toes. He is likely to knock you off your feet just being led across the yard if he can find anything to spook at, and when it comes to removing rugs he is something of a Houdini. He has little difficulty in pulling summer sheets and other light rugs straight over his head, even if there are straps under his tummy, so at night he has a rug with leg straps to keep it in place. During the day he can often be seen looking like an overgrown pit pony in a thin, rather dirty New Zealand rug which has so far survived all his attempts at removal.

Milton has lived in the same stable all the time he has been with the Whitakers. He used to be next door to Ryan's Son, but now Hopscotch is in Ryan's old stable. 'I try not to show any favouritism to the horses,' says John. 'I think you can spoil them, and Milton gets spoiled enough at the shows. I don't think he should be treated any differently from the other horses. Of course he's worth a lot of money, but you can't wrap him up in cotton wool.' So at home Milton is just one of the others, although he seems to have enough tricks up his sleeve to ensure that he gets his own way most of the time.

When Milton goes to a big international show it is a different story. He undergoes a personality change, from being just 'one of the others' at home in Yorkshire, to being show jumping's superstar. The crowds adore him, and he knows it. When he enters the arena he commands attention, initially because of his beautiful colour, but he has the presence and personality to hold audiences spellbound throughout his performances. His extravagant action, his grace, his poise and his enthusiasm combine to produce a perfect jumping machine, and people soon realise that they are watching something exceptional.

'There are a lot of things that make Milton so good, but the most important is that he wants to do it,' says John. 'He loves jumping, and he loves the atmosphere, especially at the indoor shows where it is more immediate – a packed arena with a receptive crowd seems to lift his performance. He has the scope and ability as well. When other horses are reaching their limit, Milton always seems to have a bit more in reserve.'

When people say that Milton and John are suited it is not just in their ability. They both have the right personality for the job. Under pressure, when some horses tend to fall apart, Milton responds by jumping even better, while John stays cool and professional. 'When you go into a competition that you know you can win, and you know that people expect you to win, then there is a lot more pressure on you than on someone who is less well known. I try not to think about it; I just block it all out and concentrate on what I am doing in the ring.

'At the World Cup final in Gothenburg, for example, I tried to treat each day as a normal day, doing my best in the individual classes and not worrying about the final result. Everyone gets nervous before big competitions, but I think I've learnt to control my nerves. You have to get yourself worked up a little bit, or you don't give your best.'

Both horse and rider have the calm, 'laid-back' outlook that is so necessary for the sort of life they lead. Milton has never been bothered by the constant turmoil of his worldwide travels. As long as he gets his food and sleep – 'and a bit of show jumping in between' – he is quite content. John has the enviable knack of being able to fall asleep virtually anywhere – taxis, aeroplanes, airports, hotel lounges. He travels light, sauntering from aeroplane to passport control with his hands in his pockets and, seemingly, without a care in the world, while

Exercising in the field. Milton is rarely jumped at home. He does not need any more training, and he gets plenty of jumping at the shows.

The Henderson team at Heyside Farm: (left to right) Fonda, Gammon, Grannusch, Salvador, Hopscotch and Milton. John and his brother Michael have been sponsored by Henderson Unit Trust Management since December 1989.

others struggle with bags, briefcases and duty-free, looking hot and bothered.

Milton gets bored when he travels. 'He's usually bored before the box has left Yorkshire,' says Penny, who travels to most of the shows with him. 'He gets a bit bolshie in the box, and paws at the floor. If he starts being really difficult and kicking at the partitions we sometimes have to put hobbles on him. Fortunately he is always good to load. The only things he doesn't like are the narrow ramps on to aeroplanes, so we have to get behind him with a broom. He usually travels well, but he did get a bit upset on the way back from the World Cup final in Gothenburg when we had a very rough crossing. Touch wood, I've never had to

Coming down the bank at the Falsterbo Derby in 1987, the only Derby in which Milton has competed. He finished third.

dope him on the lorry. I always carry some with me, but I hope I never have to use it because I don't think I'd get near him with the needle.'

For a horse who usually takes everything in his stride Milton has an inexplicable and very strong aversion to syringes. This creates quite a serious problem at shows because he frequently has to be dope-tested after a successful performance. 'He's had so many vets on the floor,' says Penny. 'They go to put the needle in him and he leaps forward at them. It usually takes about three people to hold him. When you have got the needle in, it's a battle to get the syringe on, and then it's difficult to get any blood out of him because he's so tense.'

Life at the shows is by no means as exciting and glamorous as it appears to the public, indeed, for much of the time the horses are cooped up in small stables. The grooms try to take them out and walk them round the showground as much as possible, but it can be very difficult at the indoor shows. In Vienna, for example, the horses are stabled in an airless, underground car park where there is no daylight. Gothenburg is even worse because of the contrast between the underground stabling, where it is too hot even to put a sheet on the horses, to the cold weather outside where they need about four rugs to keep warm.

The stables there are very small: unless the horses put their heads out to look into the gangway they literally have to stand corner to corner to fit in. At most of the shows the floors are quite slippery and the supply of wood shavings is limited, so Milton's legs are always protected with big stable bandages that

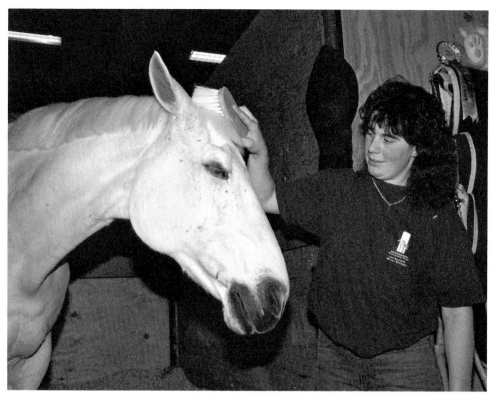

Milton has his face brushed by his groom, Penny Stevens, at Olympia.

come right over his knees. The only problem with that arrangement is that, if he gets bored during the night, the next morning his bandages will be strewn all over the box.

To give the horses a little more space the grooms usually leave the stable doors open during the day and put a chain across the gap, attached at either side by string. If no one is looking and Milton feels in need of a little entertainment, he will squeeze his way under the chain (or, if he is being particularly obstreperous, just walk straight through it, breaking the string), and then wander down the lines to have a good look round. 'He's a very nosey horse, and likes to know what's going on,' says Penny. 'If you turn your back on him, he'll be out.'

When Milton is competing, Penny walks him round for about twenty minutes before the class starts, to loosen him up. Then, when there are about ten horses to go before Milton's turn, John gets on and starts working him.

Once they enter the arena they are the focus of attention, but both horse and rider are well used to this now. One thing that does bother John, though, is the number of people using flashbulbs to take photographs. 'Sometimes when you are jumping a fence towards the crowds all you can see is a mass of flashes, and

John McEwen – British team vet

'I first met Marius, Milton's father, in 1978 when Caroline became the first woman to win a medal in the World Championships. I travelled with Marius on several occasions and also attended him at stud. Like Milton, he was a very strong and determined character and very full of his own importance. I am quite sure that this is where Milton has inherited his tendency to grow in stature whenever a big competition is in the offing.

Marius ended his days back in Gwent, and I had occasion to treat him in his latter years. Even though he was old then, he had lost none of his outward-going temperament.

I think there are three reasons why Milton has been such a successful show jumper: he is physically a very strong, athletic type of horse; he has a temperament that loves the big occasion, and he has a good rider. I have been with Milton at most of his major international championships and you can watch him grow on the day of a big competition. He loves a big crowd and he loves to perform. I think there is a bit of the showman in him. You almost get the impression when he enters the ring that he is just going to show them that he is the "greatest".

There are always two sides to every coin, and I would say that Milton's temperament, which superbly fits him to compete at the top of the tree athletically, can also make him quite a difficult fellow to handle at times. A classical instance of this is when we try to load him into crates to fly him to Canada or the USA. He can be very stubborn.

I have always felt that those who look after Milton, the Whitakers and his grooms, have a super relationship with the horse, and I am sure that a firm enough hand to keep him in his place, combined with the ability to allow him to know that he is king in his field is another aspect of the successful combination that has been created between John and Milton.'

it can be very distracting. I'm not sure that it's really ever caused us to have a fence down, but it's a good excuse to use now and then!' If they do make a mistake, John finds one of the most difficult things is to explain to everyone afterwards what went wrong. As Liz Edgar says, with a horse like Milton there is a major enquiry every time he has a fence down. 'There isn't always a good reason,' says John. 'You have to accept that horses aren't machines, and even Milton makes mistakes now and then.'

What a lot of people would like to capture on camera is Milton performing his victory party-piece, when he jumps into the air with all four feet off the ground. It is an exceptionally difficult movement to sit to, and John is not keen to experience it too frequently in case Milton starts to make a habit of it – out hacking at home, for example. John discovered quite by accident that Milton could perform this highly advanced movement. It happened at a show once after the lap of honour, when all the horses tend to get rather excited and there is a general rush for the exit. John tried to hold Milton back to allow some of the other riders to get out first, when suddenly Milton lunged 'about three feet in the air'.

'Now he does it on command,' explains John. 'If he's very excited, and he usually is during the prize-giving, I just have to hold him back and squeeze a bit. In Gothenburg, at the end of the World Cup final, we did the lap of honour and then I turned him down the centre of the arena, stopped him, held and squeezed, and he did it straight away.'

After all the excitement of the prize-giving ceremony and the lap of honour, it is not surprising that Milton returns to his stable a little agitated. 'He doesn't much like being brushed at the best of times, and he's particularly sensitive after he has been jumped,' says Penny. 'I usually leave him alone for ten minutes to let him relax, and I try to keep everyone away from him. People tend to come rushing back to his stable to see him as soon as a class has ended, and he gets

Joining in the festive mood at Olympia (1989). Milton's popularity makes it difficult to ensure that he gets enough peace and quiet in his stable when he is at a show.

Milton performing his party trick – a dramatic leap into the air – after winning the World Cup final in Gothenburg, Sweden, 1991.

miserable if he is bothered too much after a competition.'

One of the most difficult things at the shows is to ensure that Milton has some time to himself, particularly at places like Wembley, where the stable area accommodates the show horses, the ponies for the Pony Club Games, horses for displays and so on, as well as the show jumpers. The children all want to see Milton, and they tend to hang around his stable all day, feeding him Polos. If someone asks John where Milton is, he usually sends them off in the opposite direction to the stable of another grey horse. 'Milton loves the attention, but I think he needs some peace and quiet; and it can't be good for him eating Polos all day.'

Milton's programme tends to follow a similar pattern each year: during the winter he is competing on the World Cup circuit, after which there is usually a break before Hickstead and the Royal International Horse Show. Then there are the Nations Cup meetings and other international shows, including the usual trip to Calgary in September, finishing with the Horse of the Year Show at Wembley. After that, the World Cup circuit starts again. It is a tough schedule, but John rarely jumps Milton in more than three classes at a show, so he is kept as fresh as possible for the main competitions. Mr and Mrs Bradley do not try to control Milton's programme, but they have told John that they do not want the horse taken down the Hickstead Bank or ridden in puissance classes.

'I have taken Milton into one or two puissance competitions but only to jump a couple of rounds, as I think it does all horses good to jump something a bit bigger and more solid than usual, just to make them think about what they are doing. But I would never have any intention of trying to win a puissance with him. When you keep pushing a horse to jump higher and higher, as you do in a puissance competition, at some point they are going to reach their limit, and once a horse has found his limit he is never quite the same again; his self-belief goes.

'I think Hopscotch found his limit in Aachen, in the World Championships [1986]. I had won the European individual bronze medal with him in Dinard the previous year, and at that time he was jumping very boldly. Then I took him a stage further to the World Championships, where he was confronted with something that he could not jump and it frightened him. He is still very good now, but he has never had quite the same confidence again.'

The Bradleys, who are as concerned as John over Milton's well-being, dislike the idea of Milton competing in the Hickstead Derby because of the risk of the descent down the 10ft 6in bank. John hopes that one day they may change their minds because he thinks Milton would be good at the Derby. 'Milton's a sensible horse, and he does listen, so I don't think he would do anything stupid at the bank. He'd be quite capable of winning the Hickstead Derby.'

At the age of fourteen Milton is still jumping as effortlessly as he was three years ago and has lost none of his enthusiasm for the sport, a reflection of the care and good management that he has received throughout his life. As a youngster he was fortunate to have come into the hands of a horsewoman of Caroline Bradley's calibre, whose painstaking efforts with his early education and training gave him the best possible start to his career. A brief spell with Steve Hadley was followed by a year and a half off work; and since then he has been with John, who certainly could not be accused of overworking his horses. 'There's no reason why he should not keep going for a few years yet,' says John. 'I shall probably ease back a bit more on him in a year or two, do fewer shows and just put him into the competitions that suit him best. But I'll take it from year to year.'

One suspects that if Milton has his way he will continue to thrill audiences with his brilliant performances for as long as possible. After all, that's what he likes doing best.

John avoids having his ear nibbled. Milton can't be totally trusted not to have an occasional nip. 'He's quite affectionate, though not in the way a dog might be,' says John. 'He certainly knows what's going on; he knows me and the people who look after him.'

MILTON'S MAJOR WINS

1985 – World Cup Qualifier, Bordeaux

1986 – Grand Prix, Royal International Horse Show
Grand Prix, Calgary

1987 – Grand Prix, Gothenburg
Grand Prix, Rotterdam
Team gold medal and individual silver at European Championships, St Gallen
World Cup Qualifier, New York

1988 – World Cup Qualifier, Paris
Grand Prix, Dortmund
World Cup Qualifier, S'Hertogenbosch
Grand Prix, Royal International Horse Show
Grand Prix, Zurich
International Masters, Horse of the Year Show
Grand Prix, Stuttgart
World Cup Qualifier, Brussels

1989 – Grand Prix, Dortmund
World Cup Qualifier, Geneva
World Cup European League
Grand Prix, Cannes
Team and individual gold medals at European Championships, Rotterdam
International Masters, Horse of the Year Show
Grand Prix, Frankfurt

1990 – World Cup Qualifier, Paris
World Cup Qualifier, S'Hertogenbosch
Grand Prix, Gothenburg
World Cup Final, Dortmund
World Cup European League
King George V Gold Cup, Royal International Horse Show
Team bronze and individual silver at World Championships, Stockholm
International Masters, Horse of the Year Show

1991 – World Cup Final, Gothenburg
Grand Prix, Hickstead

MILTON'S NATIONS CUP RECORD

	ROUND 1 Faults	ROUND 2 Faults	JUMP-OFF Faults
1986 – Hickstead	12.75	5.5	
Rotterdam	0.25	0.50	
Calgary	0	0	0
1987 – Hickstead	4	0.25	
Aachen	0	0	4
Falsterbo	4.25	0	0
Dublin	0	NP	
Rotterdam	0	0	
St Gallen (European Chmps)	0	0.50	
Calgary	0	NP	
Toronto	0	0	
1988 – Hickstead	0	0	
1989 – Hickstead	0	0	
Rotterdam (European Chmps)	4	4	
Calgary	0	0	
1990 – Hickstead	0	0	
Stockholm (World Chmps)	4.05	4	
Calgary	0	NP	
1991 – Hickstead	0	0	
Aachen	0	0	

INTERESTING FACTS ABOUT MILTON

- Milton has won over £900,000 in prize-money.
- He has been the top prize-money winner in Britain since 1986.
- He had won thirteen Grands Prix and eight World Cup qualifiers up to July 1991.
- He is one of only two horses to have won the World Cup final in two consecutive years.
- Up to July 1991 Milton had won eleven Volvos and a Mercedes, and had contributed towards numerous other car prizes.
- He has had only two refusals in his life: one in Bordeaux and one at Wembley.
- He has won the International Masters competition at Wembley's Horse of the Year Show for three consecutive years, 1988–1990.
- He has jumped thirteen double clear rounds in Nations Cups between 1986 and July 1991.
- He is 16.2hh but grows in stature when he enters a crowded arena.
- In seven years with John Whitaker he has had only one illness that has prevented him from competing.

MILTON'S PRIZE-MONEY RECORD

Milton has been the top prize-money winner in Britain every year since 1986.

Winnings

1986 – £71,617
1987 – £91,742
1988 – £144,298
1989 – £206,729
1990 – £182,737